BROKEN, NOT BEATEN

Winning Over Post Traumatic Stress

Dr Bhaskar Bora

TABLE OF CONTENTS:

CHAPTER 1: INTRODUCTION

Post-Traumatic Stress Disorder (PTSD) is a mental health condition that is triggered by experiencing or witnessing a traumatic event. While it is commonly associated with war veterans, PTSD can affect anyone who has been through a harrowing experience, such as natural disasters, serious accidents, terrorist acts, rape, or other violent personal assaults. The condition manifests in various ways and can have profound impacts on an individual's life.

PTSD is characterized by four main types of symptoms:

1. Intrusive Thoughts: These are unwanted memories, nightmares, or flashbacks of the traumatic event that can make the individual feel as though they are reliving the experience. These intrusive thoughts can be triggered by reminders of the trauma, such as certain sounds, sights, or smells.

2. Avoidance: People with PTSD may go to great lengths to avoid places, people, activities, or situations that remind them of the traumatic event. This avoidance can disrupt daily life and prevent individuals from engaging in activities they once enjoyed.

3. Negative Changes in Thoughts and Mood: This can include feelings of hopelessness, memory problems, difficulty maintaining close relationships, and a loss of interest in activities previously enjoyed. Individuals may also experience negative thoughts about themselves or others and may struggle

with feelings of detachment or numbness.

4. Changes in Physical and Emotional Reactions: These symptoms, also known as arousal symptoms, include being easily startled, feeling tense or "on edge," difficulty sleeping, and angry outbursts. These reactions can interfere with daily tasks and make it difficult for individuals to concentrate or relax.

The development of PTSD can be influenced by a variety of factors. Some people may develop symptoms soon after a traumatic event, while others may not experience symptoms until months or even years later. The risk of developing PTSD can be affected by the nature of the trauma, the individual's history of mental health issues, their coping mechanisms, and the support they receive from friends and family.

Understanding the neurobiology of PTSD can shed light on why some people develop the disorder while others do not. Trauma can alter brain functions, particularly in areas like the amygdala, hippocampus, and prefrontal cortex. The amygdala is responsible for processing emotions and is often overactive in people with PTSD, leading to heightened fear and anxiety responses. The hippocampus, which plays a key role in memory formation, may become smaller and less effective, affecting the individual's ability to distinguish between past and present threats. The prefrontal cortex, involved in decision-making and regulating emotions, may become less active, making it difficult for individuals to manage their emotional responses.

There are many misconceptions about PTSD. One common myth is that PTSD only affects soldiers. In reality, anyone who has experienced a traumatic event can develop PTSD. Another misconception is that PTSD is a sign of weakness. However, PTSD is a complex psychological response to trauma, not a character flaw. Understanding these myths and the reality of PTSD is crucial for supporting those who suffer from this condition.

Meet Sarah, a dedicated nurse who worked in a busy city hospital. During a particularly harrowing shift, a patient she was caring for passed away suddenly and violently. Despite her best efforts, Sarah was unable to save him. The experience left her shaken, but she continued to work, believing that she could handle the emotional aftermath. Months later, she began to experience nightmares, flashbacks, and an overwhelming sense of guilt and helplessness. Sarah's once thriving career began to suffer as she struggled to maintain her composure at work. She avoided the hospital room where the incident occurred and became increasingly isolated from her colleagues. It wasn't until a close friend noticed her distress and urged her to seek help that Sarah began her journey towards understanding and managing her PTSD.

CHAPTER 2: UNDERSTANDING PTSD

To fully grasp the nature of PTSD, it is essential to understand the various causes and triggers that can lead to its development. PTSD can result from a wide range of traumatic experiences, and the severity of the symptoms often correlates with the intensity of the trauma.

Causes and Triggers of PTSD:

1. Combat and Military Exposure: Many military personnel who have been in combat situations are at high risk for developing PTSD. The constant threat of danger, witnessing the death or injury of comrades, and the stress of combat can leave lasting psychological scars.

2. Childhood Trauma: Early childhood experiences, such as physical, emotional, or sexual abuse, can predispose individuals to PTSD. The impact of these experiences can be long-lasting and affect emotional and psychological development.

3. Natural Disasters: Survivors of natural disasters such as earthquakes, hurricanes, or floods may develop PTSD due to the sudden and life-threatening nature of these events. The loss of homes, loved ones, and the sense of safety can be profoundly traumatic.

4. Accidents: Serious accidents, including car crashes, workplace incidents, or other life-threatening situations, can trigger PTSD. The suddenness and severity of these events can leave individuals feeling vulnerable and fearful.

5. Violence and Assault: Being a victim of violence, such as robbery, assault, or domestic abuse, can lead to PTSD. The sense of violation and loss of control in these situations can be overwhelming.

6. Medical Emergencies: Severe illness or injury, especially if life-threatening, can result in PTSD. The trauma of medical procedures, hospitalizations, and the fear of death can be significant stressors.

Understanding the science behind PTSD involves exploring how traumatic experiences impact the brain and body. The stress response system, which includes the hypothalamus, pituitary gland, and adrenal glands, plays a critical role in how we react to stress. In individuals with PTSD, this system becomes dysregulated, leading to an overactive stress response even in non-threatening situations.

The Neurobiology of PTSD:

1. The Amygdala: This part of the brain is responsible for processing emotions, particularly fear and aggression. In people with PTSD, the amygdala becomes hyperactive, causing heightened fear responses and emotional reactivity.
2. The Hippocampus: This region is crucial for forming and retrieving memories. PTSD can cause the hippocampus to shrink, making it difficult for individuals to differentiate between past and present threats and leading to flashbacks and intrusive memories.

3. The Prefrontal Cortex: This area of the brain is involved in decision-making, impulse control, and regulating emotions. PTSD can impair the functioning of the prefrontal cortex,

making it challenging for individuals to manage their emotions and reactions.

The body's stress hormones, such as cortisol and adrenaline, also play a role in PTSD. Chronic stress can lead to elevated levels of these hormones, which can have damaging effects on the brain and body over time.

Common Misconceptions and Myths:

There are several misconceptions about PTSD that can hinder understanding and support for those affected. One prevalent myth is that PTSD only affects individuals immediately after a traumatic event. In reality, symptoms can emerge months or even years later. Another myth is that PTSD is a sign of weakness or an inability to cope. However, PTSD is a complex psychological condition that requires understanding and appropriate treatment, not judgment.

John, a firefighter, had been a first responder for over a decade. He was accustomed to high-stress situations and believed he could handle anything. However, after rescuing a child from a devastating house fire, John began experiencing nightmares and flashbacks of the incident. The child's face haunted him, and he found it increasingly difficult to go to work. John tried to push through the symptoms, but they only worsened. It wasn't until he attended a support group for first responders that he began to understand his condition and seek help.

The journey to a PTSD diagnosis is often a difficult and confusing one. Many individuals do not recognize the symptoms in themselves or may attribute their feelings to other factors. Understanding the signs and seeking professional help is crucial for effective management and recovery.

Recognizing the Signs in Oneself and Others:

1. Emotional Symptoms: Persistent feelings of fear, anxiety, and

sadness are common. Individuals may also experience intense anger, guilt, or shame related to the traumatic event.

2. Behavioral Changes: Avoidance of places, people, or activities that remind them of the trauma. This can lead to social withdrawal and isolation.

3. Cognitive Symptoms: Difficulty concentrating, memory problems, and negative thoughts about oneself and the world. Individuals may also have distorted beliefs about the trauma and its consequences.

4. Physical Symptoms: Sleep disturbances, including insomnia and nightmares, are frequent. Other physical symptoms can include fatigue, muscle tension, and a heightened startle response.

The Importance of Early Diagnosis:

Early diagnosis of PTSD can significantly improve the prognosis. The sooner individuals seek help, the more effective the treatment can be in managing symptoms and preventing them from worsening. Early intervention can also help individuals understand their condition and develop coping strategies.

Seeking Professional Help:

Professional help for PTSD typically involves a combination of therapy and medication. Therapists who specialize in trauma can provide invaluable support and guidance. Finding the right therapist and building a trusting relationship is a critical step in the healing process.

Emily, a survivor of a severe car accident, began experiencing flashbacks and panic attacks months after the incident. She initially dismissed these symptoms, believing they were normal reactions to her trauma. However, when her anxiety began interfering with her daily life, Emily sought help from a therapist. Through therapy, she learned to recognize and manage her symptoms, ultimately regaining control of her life.

Overcoming the Stigma:

One of the biggest barriers to seeking help for PTSD is the stigma associated with mental health issues. Many individuals feel ashamed or embarrassed to admit they are struggling, fearing judgment from others. Overcoming this stigma is crucial for accessing the support and treatment needed for recovery. Educating oneself and others about PTSD and mental health can help reduce stigma and encourage more people to seek help.

Mark, a military veteran, struggled with PTSD for years after returning from deployment. He felt ashamed to admit he needed help, believing that doing so would make him appear weak. It wasn't until a fellow veteran shared his own experiences with PTSD and encouraged Mark to seek help that he finally reached out to a therapist. Mark's journey to recovery began when he overcame the stigma and sought the support he needed.

Therapy plays a crucial role in the treatment of PTSD. Various therapeutic approaches can help individuals process their trauma and develop healthy coping mechanisms. Understanding the different types of therapy available can help individuals find the right fit for their needs.

Types of Therapy Available:

1. Cognitive Behavioral Therapy (CBT): CBT is one of the most effective treatments for PTSD. It involves identifying and challenging negative thought patterns and behaviors related to the trauma. CBT helps individuals develop healthier ways of thinking and reacting to traumatic memories.

2. Exposure Therapy: This form of therapy helps individuals confront their fears and memories related to the trauma in a controlled environment. By gradually facing these fears, individuals can reduce their anxiety and distress over time.

3. Eye Movement Desensitization and Reprocessing (EMDR): EMDR is a unique therapy that involves recalling traumatic memories while focusing on external stimuli, such as side-to-side eye movements. This process helps reprocess the trauma and reduce its emotional impact.

4. Group Therapy: Group therapy provides a supportive environment where individuals can share their experiences with others who have similar struggles. This sense of community and understanding can be incredibly healing.

5. Narrative Exposure Therapy (NET): NET involves creating a detailed narrative of the traumatic event and processing it with the therapist. This helps integrate the traumatic memories into the individual's life story, reducing their emotional power.

Lisa, a survivor of domestic abuse, found solace in group therapy. Initially hesitant to share her experiences, Lisa was surprised by the support and understanding she received from others in the group. Through sharing and listening to others, she found strength and began to heal from her trauma.

Finding the Right Therapist:

Choosing the right therapist is an important step in the healing process. It is essential to find a therapist who specializes in trauma and PTSD and with whom the individual feels comfortable. Building a trusting relationship with the therapist can make a significant difference in the effectiveness of the treatment.

David, who had been struggling with PTSD after a workplace accident, went through several therapists before finding the right fit. His persistence paid off when he finally found a therapist who understood his needs and helped him navigate his recovery journey.

In addition to therapy, medication can play a vital role in

managing PTSD symptoms. While medication is not a cure for PTSD, it can help reduce the severity of symptoms and improve the overall quality of life for those affected.

Understanding the Role of Medication:

Medications for PTSD are typically used to manage symptoms such as anxiety, depression, and insomnia. They can help individuals feel more stable and capable of engaging in therapy and other treatments.
Common Medications Prescribed:

1. Selective Serotonin Reuptake Inhibitors (SSRIs): SSRIs, such as sertraline (Zoloft) and paroxetine (Paxil), are commonly prescribed to treat PTSD. They work by increasing the levels of serotonin in the brain, which can help improve mood and reduce anxiety.

2. Serotonin-Norepinephrine Reuptake Inhibitors (SNRIs): SNRIs, such as venlafaxine (Effexor), can also be effective in treating PTSD by increasing both serotonin and norepinephrine levels.

3. Prazosin: This medication is often prescribed to help reduce nightmares and improve sleep in individuals with PTSD.

4. Antipsychotics: In some cases, antipsychotic medications may be prescribed to help manage severe anxiety or depression.

Managing Side Effects:

As with any medication, there can be side effects. It is important for individuals to work closely with their healthcare provider to monitor and manage any side effects. Regular follow-up appointments can help ensure that the medication is working effectively and that any side effects are addressed promptly.

Combining Medication with Therapy:

For many individuals, the most effective approach to treating

PTSD involves a combination of medication and therapy. Medication can help manage symptoms, making it easier for individuals to engage in therapy and address the underlying trauma. This holistic approach can provide comprehensive support for recovery.

Karen, a survivor of a terrorist attack, found that combining medication with therapy was the key to her recovery. The medication helped stabilize her mood and reduce her anxiety, allowing her to fully participate in therapy and work through her trauma.

By understanding PTSD, its symptoms, and the available treatments, individuals can take the first steps towards recovery. The journey may be challenging, but with the right support and resources, it is possible to turn adversity into opportunity and build a fulfilling life.

CHAPTER 3: THE ROLE OF THERAPY

Therapy plays a crucial role in the treatment of PTSD, offering individuals a pathway to understand and manage their symptoms. Various therapeutic approaches are available, each designed to address different aspects of trauma and recovery. Understanding the types of therapy available can help individuals make informed decisions about their treatment options.

Types of Therapy Available:

1. Cognitive Behavioral Therapy (CBT): CBT is one of the most widely used and effective treatments for PTSD. It focuses on identifying and changing negative thought patterns and behaviors that contribute to distress. By addressing these cognitive distortions, individuals can develop healthier ways of thinking and coping with their trauma.

2. Exposure Therapy: This form of therapy involves exposing individuals to their traumatic memories or triggers in a controlled environment. The goal is to reduce the power these memories or triggers have over the individual. By gradually facing their fears, individuals can desensitize themselves to the trauma and reduce their anxiety.

3. Eye Movement Desensitization and Reprocessing (EMDR): EMDR is a unique therapy that involves recalling traumatic memories while simultaneously engaging in bilateral

stimulation, such as side-to-side eye movements. This process helps reprocess the traumatic memories, making them less distressing over time.

4. Narrative Exposure Therapy (NET): NET involves creating a detailed narrative of the traumatic event and processing it with the therapist. This approach helps integrate the traumatic memories into the individual's life story, reducing their emotional impact.

5. Psychodynamic Therapy: This approach focuses on exploring the unconscious mind and understanding how past experiences shape current behavior. It aims to uncover hidden emotions and conflicts that contribute to PTSD symptoms.

6. Mindfulness-Based Therapies: These therapies incorporate mindfulness practices, such as meditation and yoga, to help individuals stay present and manage their anxiety. Mindfulness can be particularly helpful in reducing hyperarousal and improving emotional regulation.

7. Group Therapy and Support Groups: Group therapy provides a supportive environment where individuals can share their experiences and learn from others who have faced similar challenges. Support groups can offer a sense of community and validation, which is crucial for healing.

Maria, a survivor of childhood abuse, found herself struggling with intense anxiety and depression as an adult. After trying various medications without success, she decided to explore therapy. Her therapist recommended Cognitive Behavioral Therapy (CBT), which helped Maria identify and challenge the negative beliefs she had about herself. Through CBT, Maria learned to develop healthier thought patterns and coping mechanisms, significantly improving her quality of life.

Therapy offers a diverse range of approaches to help individuals manage PTSD. By finding the right type of therapy, individuals can begin to heal and reclaim their lives from the grip of trauma.

Cognitive Behavioral Therapy (CBT)

Cognitive Behavioral Therapy (CBT) is a highly effective and evidence-based treatment for PTSD. CBT focuses on identifying and changing the negative thought patterns and behaviors that contribute to PTSD symptoms. It helps individuals develop healthier ways of thinking and coping with their trauma.

Key Components of CBT for PTSD:

1. Identifying Negative Thoughts: One of the core aspects of CBT is helping individuals identify the negative thoughts and beliefs that are contributing to their distress. These thoughts often stem from the trauma and can include feelings of guilt, shame, and helplessness.
2. Challenging Cognitive Distortions: Once negative thoughts are identified, the therapist works with the individual to challenge these cognitive distortions. This involves examining the evidence for and against these thoughts and developing more balanced and realistic perspectives.

3. Developing Coping Strategies: CBT teaches individuals practical coping strategies to manage their symptoms. This can include relaxation techniques, problem-solving skills, and strategies for dealing with triggers.

4. Exposure Techniques: CBT often incorporates exposure techniques to help individuals confront and desensitize themselves to their traumatic memories or triggers. This can be done through imaginal exposure (revisiting the trauma in a safe, controlled way) or in vivo exposure (gradually facing real-life situations that are feared or avoided).

5. Behavioral Activation: This aspect of CBT focuses on helping individuals engage in activities they have been avoiding due to their PTSD symptoms. By gradually increasing engagement in positive activities, individuals can improve their mood and

overall functioning.

6. Building Resilience: CBT also aims to build resilience by helping individuals develop a sense of control over their thoughts and behaviors. This can involve setting goals, building self-esteem, and learning to cope with stress in healthy ways.

After witnessing a traumatic incident at work, Jake developed severe anxiety and nightmares. He found it difficult to concentrate and began avoiding situations that reminded him of the event. Jake's therapist introduced him to CBT, where he learned to identify and challenge his negative thoughts about the trauma. Through exposure therapy, Jake gradually confronted his fears and learned to manage his anxiety. Over time, he regained his confidence and was able to return to work.

CBT is a powerful tool in the treatment of PTSD. By addressing the cognitive and behavioural aspects of the disorder, CBT helps individuals regain control over their lives and move towards recovery.

Eye Movement Desensitization and Reprocessing (EMDR)

Eye Movement Desensitization and Reprocessing (EMDR) is a unique and highly effective therapy for PTSD. EMDR involves recalling traumatic memories while simultaneously engaging in bilateral stimulation, such as side-to-side eye movements. This process helps reprocess the traumatic memories, making them less distressing over time.

How EMDR Works:

1. Assessment and Preparation: The first phase of EMDR involves assessing the individual's history and preparing them for the therapy. The therapist gathers information about the trauma and explains the EMDR process. This phase also includes teaching relaxation techniques to help manage anxiety during the sessions.

2. Identifying Target Memories: The therapist and individual

work together to identify the specific memories or aspects of the trauma that will be the focus of the EMDR sessions. These target memories are typically the most distressing and impactful aspects of the trauma.

3. Desensitization: During the desensitization phase, the individual recalls the traumatic memory while following the therapist's finger or another object with their eyes. This bilateral stimulation can also involve tapping or auditory tones. The process helps reduce the emotional intensity of the memory and allows the individual to reprocess the trauma.

4. Installation: In this phase, positive beliefs and feelings are reinforced to replace the negative ones associated with the trauma. The individual focuses on these positive thoughts while continuing the bilateral stimulation.

5. Body Scan: The therapist asks the individual to focus on any residual physical sensations related to the trauma. This helps identify any remaining distress and addresses it through further bilateral stimulation.

6. Closure: Each EMDR session ends with closure to ensure the individual feels stable and safe. The therapist may teach additional coping strategies or relaxation techniques to use between sessions.

7. Re-evaluation: In subsequent sessions, the therapist reevaluates the individual's progress and identifies any new target memories or issues that need to be addressed. This ensures the therapy remains effective and responsive to the individual's needs.

Anna, a survivor of a violent assault, struggled with intense flashbacks and nightmares. Traditional talk therapy did not seem to alleviate her symptoms. Her therapist suggested EMDR, and Anna decided to give it a try. During the EMDR sessions, Anna was able to recall and process the traumatic memories in a new way. The bilateral stimulation helped reduce the emotional intensity of the memories, and over time, her flashbacks and nightmares diminished. EMDR provided Anna with a sense of relief and allowed her to move forward in her healing journey.

EMDR is a powerful therapy that can help individuals reprocess traumatic memories and reduce their emotional impact. By incorporating bilateral stimulation, EMDR provides a unique approach to healing from PTSD.

Group Therapy and Support Groups

Group therapy and support groups provide a supportive environment where individuals with PTSD can share their experiences and learn from others who have faced similar challenges. These group settings offer a sense of community and validation, which is crucial for healing.

Benefits of Group Therapy and Support Groups:

1. Shared Experiences: One of the most significant benefits of group therapy and support groups is the opportunity to connect with others who have experienced similar traumas. Sharing experiences and hearing others' stories can provide a sense of validation and reduce feelings of isolation.

2. Supportive Environment: Group settings offer a safe and supportive environment where individuals can express their thoughts and emotions without fear of judgment. This support can foster a sense of belonging and acceptance.

3. Learning from Others: Group members can learn from each other's experiences and coping strategies. Hearing how others have managed their symptoms and navigated their recovery journey can provide valuable insights and inspiration.

4. Building Social Connections: Group therapy and support groups can help individuals build new social connections and

friendships. These connections can provide ongoing support and encouragement outside of the group sessions.

5. Improving Communication Skills: Participating in group therapy can help individuals improve their communication and interpersonal skills. This can be particularly beneficial for those who have withdrawn from social interactions due to their PTSD symptoms.

6. Accountability and Motivation: Group members can provide accountability and motivation to each other. Knowing that others are on a similar journey can encourage individuals to stay committed to their treatment and recovery goals.

After a traumatic experience, Linda felt isolated and struggled to cope with her symptoms. She decided to join a support group for trauma survivors. In the group, Linda found a sense of community and understanding that she had been missing. Hearing others' stories and sharing her own helped her feel less alone in her struggles. The support group became a crucial part of Linda's recovery, providing her with the encouragement and motivation she needed to heal.

Group therapy and support groups offer a unique and valuable form of support for individuals with PTSD. By connecting with others who have faced similar challenges, individuals can find strength, understanding, and hope in their recovery journey.

Finding the Right Therapist

John had always considered himself a resilient person. As a firefighter, he had faced numerous life-threatening situations and witnessed countless tragedies. However, after a particularly harrowing rescue where he was unable to save a young child, John found himself struggling with overwhelming guilt and flashbacks. His once unshakable confidence was replaced with anxiety and self-doubt.

John knew he needed help but was unsure where to start. He decided to seek therapy but felt apprehensive about finding the right therapist. After several unsuccessful attempts with different therapists, John began to feel discouraged. Each session left him feeling more frustrated and misunderstood.

Determined to find relief, John continued his search and eventually found a therapist who specialized in trauma and PTSD. From their first session, John felt a sense of trust and connection. The therapist took the time to understand his experiences and validate his feelings. Together, they developed a treatment plan that included Cognitive Behavioral Therapy (CBT) and Eye Movement Desensitization and Reprocessing (EMDR).

Through CBT, John learned to identify and challenge the negative thoughts that were fuelling his guilt and anxiety. EMDR sessions helped him process the traumatic memories in a new way, reducing their emotional intensity. Over time, John began to see improvements in his symptoms and felt a renewed sense of hope.

Finding the right therapist made all the difference in John's recovery. He realized that therapy is not a one-size-fits-all approach and that it was essential to find a therapist who understood his unique needs. With the right support, John was able to regain his confidence and return to his work with a new perspective.

John's story highlights the importance of perseverance in finding the right therapist. It can be a challenging journey, but the right therapist can provide the understanding, support, and guidance needed to navigate the path to healing.

CHAPTER 4:
MEDICATION
AND PTSD

Medication can play a vital role in the treatment of PTSD, helping to manage symptoms and improve the quality of life for those affected. While medication is not a cure for PTSD, it can be an important component of a comprehensive treatment plan.

Understanding the Role of Medication:

1. Symptom Management: Medications can help manage a range of PTSD symptoms, including anxiety, depression, insomnia, and hyperarousal. By alleviating these symptoms, medication can make it easier for individuals to engage in therapy and other treatments.

2. Stabilization: For individuals experiencing severe symptoms, medication can provide stabilization, allowing them to regain a sense of normalcy and control. This stabilization can be crucial in the early stages of treatment.

3. Complementary to Therapy: Medication is often used in conjunction with therapy. While therapy addresses the underlying trauma and teaches coping strategies, medication can help manage the physiological and emotional symptoms that may hinder progress in therapy.

4. Short-Term and Long-Term Use: The use of medication

can vary from short-term to long-term, depending on the individual's needs and response to treatment. Some individuals may only need medication temporarily, while others may benefit from long-term use.

5. Individualized Treatment: The decision to use medication and the choice of specific medications should be tailored to the individual's unique needs and circumstances. This personalized approach ensures the most effective and appropriate treatment.

Lisa, a survivor of a traumatic assault, found herself struggling with intense anxiety and insomnia. Despite her efforts in therapy, she could not manage her symptoms effectively. Her therapist recommended considering medication as part of her treatment plan. With the guidance of her psychiatrist, Lisa started taking an antidepressant that helped reduce her anxiety and improve her sleep. This stabilization allowed her to fully engage in therapy and make significant progress in her recovery.

Medication can be a valuable tool in managing PTSD symptoms and supporting the overall treatment process. Understanding its role and working closely with healthcare providers can help individuals make informed decisions about their treatment.

Common Medications Prescribed

Several types of medications are commonly prescribed to help manage the symptoms of PTSD. Each medication works differently and may be more suitable for certain individuals based on their specific symptoms and needs.

1. Selective Serotonin Reuptake Inhibitors (SSRIs): SSRIs are a class of antidepressants that are commonly used to treat PTSD. They work by increasing the levels of serotonin in the brain, which can help improve mood and reduce anxiety. Common SSRIs prescribed for PTSD include sertraline (Zoloft) and paroxetine (Paxil).

2. Serotonin-Norepinephrine Reuptake Inhibitors (SNRIs):

SNRIs are another class of antidepressants that can be effective in treating PTSD. They increase the levels of both serotonin and norepinephrine in the brain. Venlafaxine (Effexor) is a commonly prescribed SNRI for PTSD.

3. Prazosin: Prazosin is a medication that is often used to treat nightmares and sleep disturbances associated with PTSD. It works by blocking the effects of adrenaline, which can help reduce the severity of nightmares and improve sleep quality.

4. Benzodiazepines: Benzodiazepines are sedative medications that can help manage anxiety and insomnia. However, they are generally prescribed with caution due to the potential for dependence and tolerance. Benzodiazepines are typically used for short-term relief of severe symptoms.

5. Antipsychotics: In some cases, antipsychotic medications may be prescribed to help manage severe anxiety, agitation, or symptoms of psychosis that can accompany PTSD. These medications can help stabilize mood and reduce extreme emotional responses.

6. Mood Stabilizers: Mood stabilizers, such as lithium or valproate, may be prescribed to help manage mood swings and emotional instability in individuals with PTSD. These medications can help create a more balanced emotional state.

After experiencing a traumatic event, Mark struggled with severe nightmares and flashbacks. His psychiatrist prescribed prazosin to help manage his nightmares. Within a few weeks, Mark noticed a significant improvement in his sleep quality and a reduction in the frequency and intensity of his nightmares. This allowed him to feel more rested and better able to cope with his daytime symptoms.

Understanding the different types of medications available and their potential benefits can help individuals and their healthcare providers make informed decisions about their treatment options.

Managing Side Effects

While medications can be highly effective in managing PTSD symptoms, they can also come with side effects. It is important for individuals to be aware of potential side effects and to work closely with their healthcare providers to manage them.

Common Side Effects and How to Manage Them:

1. Nausea and Gastrointestinal Issues: Some medications, particularly antidepressants, can cause nausea, stomach upset, or diarrhoea. Taking medications with food or adjusting the timing of the dose can help reduce these side effects. In some cases, the body may adjust to the medication over time, and these side effects may diminish.

2. Drowsiness and Fatigue: Sedative medications, such as benzodiazepines, can cause drowsiness and fatigue. It may be helpful to take these medications in the evening or before bedtime. If drowsiness is severe, it is important to discuss this with the healthcare provider, as a dosage adjustment or a different medication may be needed.

3. Insomnia: Paradoxically, some medications can cause insomnia or disrupt sleep patterns. If insomnia is an issue, the healthcare provider may recommend adjusting the timing of the dose or adding a sleep aid to the treatment plan.

4. Weight Gain: Certain medications, particularly some antidepressants and antipsychotics, can lead to weight gain. Maintaining a healthy diet and regular exercise can help manage this side effect. It is important to discuss any significant weight changes with the healthcare provider.

5. Sexual Side Effects: Some medications can cause sexual side effects, such as decreased libido or difficulty achieving orgasm. Open communication with the healthcare provider is crucial, as

they may adjust the medication or dosage to alleviate these side effects.

6. Dry Mouth: Dry mouth is a common side effect of many medications. Drinking plenty of water, chewing sugar-free gum, or using saliva substitutes can help manage this symptom.

7. Dizziness and Light-headedness: Some medications can cause dizziness or light-headedness, particularly when standing up quickly. Taking the medication at bedtime or rising slowly from a seated or lying position can help reduce these side effects.

After starting an SSRI to manage her PTSD symptoms, Emily experienced nausea and dizziness. She worked closely with her healthcare provider to adjust the timing of her medication and incorporated small, frequent meals into her diet. Over time, her body adjusted to the medication, and the side effects diminished, allowing her to focus on her recovery.

Managing side effects effectively involves open communication with healthcare providers and a willingness to adjust as needed. By addressing side effects promptly, individuals can continue their treatment with minimal disruption to their daily lives.

Combining Medication with Therapy

For many individuals with PTSD, the most effective approach to treatment involves a combination of medication and therapy. This holistic approach addresses both the physiological and psychological aspects of the disorder, providing comprehensive support for recovery.

Benefits of Combining Medication with Therapy:

1. Enhanced Symptom Management: Medication can help stabilize symptoms, such as anxiety and depression, making it easier for individuals to engage in therapy. This stabilization allows them to focus more effectively on the therapeutic process.

2. Addressing Underlying Trauma: While medication manages the symptoms, therapy addresses the underlying trauma that contributes to PTSD. Therapeutic approaches, such as Cognitive Behavioral Therapy (CBT) or Eye Movement Desensitization and Reprocessing (EMDR), help individuals process and heal from their traumatic experiences.

3. Developing Coping Strategies: Therapy provides individuals with practical coping strategies to manage their symptoms and reduce the impact of triggers. These strategies can complement the symptom relief provided by medication.

4. Improving Treatment Adherence: The combination of medication and therapy can improve treatment adherence by providing multiple avenues of support. Individuals may feel more motivated to continue their treatment when they see improvements in both their symptoms and their ability to cope.

5. Comprehensive Support: A combined approach offers comprehensive support, addressing both the mind and body. This holistic treatment plan can lead to more sustainable and long-term recovery outcomes.

David, a military veteran, struggled with severe PTSD symptoms, including flashbacks and hyperarousal. His psychiatrist prescribed an SSRI to help manage his anxiety and depression. At the same time, David began working with a therapist who specialized in trauma. Through EMDR therapy, David was able to process his traumatic memories and develop healthier coping mechanisms. The combination of medication and therapy provided David with the stability and support he needed to regain control of his life.

Combining medication with therapy can offer a powerful and comprehensive approach to treating PTSD. By addressing both the physiological and psychological aspects of the disorder, individuals can achieve more effective and lasting recovery.

Balancing Treatment Options

Karen had always been a vibrant and outgoing person, but after surviving a natural disaster, she found herself overwhelmed by fear and anxiety. Her once joyful demeanour was replaced by constant vigilance and a pervasive sense of dread. Determined to reclaim her life, Karen sought help from a mental health professional.

Karen's psychiatrist recommended a combination of medication and therapy to address her PTSD symptoms. She started taking an SSRI to help manage her anxiety and depression. The medication provided some relief, but Karen knew she needed additional support to fully heal from her trauma.

Her therapist introduced her to Cognitive Behavioral Therapy (CBT) and Eye Movement Desensitization and Reprocessing (EMDR). Through CBT, Karen learned to identify and challenge the negative thoughts that were contributing to her anxiety. EMDR sessions helped her process the traumatic memories in a new way, reducing their emotional impact.

Karen's journey was not without challenges. She experienced side effects from the medication, including nausea and insomnia. However, by working closely with her healthcare providers, she was able to adjust her treatment plan. Her psychiatrist adjusted her medication dosage, and her therapist taught her relaxation techniques to improve her sleep.

The combination of medication and therapy provided Karen with a balanced approach to her treatment. The medication helped stabilize her symptoms, while therapy addressed the underlying trauma and equipped her with practical coping strategies. Over time, Karen began to see significant improvements in her symptoms and regained her sense of joy and confidence.

Karen's story highlights the importance of finding the right balance in treatment options. By combining medication with therapy and making necessary adjustments, individuals can achieve more comprehensive and effective recovery outcomes.

CHAPTER 5: SELF-HELP STRATEGIES

Self-help strategies can play a significant role in managing PTSD and supporting overall mental health. These strategies empower individuals to take an active role in their recovery and complement professional treatment. Among the most effective self-help approaches are mindfulness and meditation.

Mindfulness and Meditation:

1. Understanding Mindfulness: Mindfulness involves paying deliberate attention to the present moment without judgment. It helps individuals become more aware of their thoughts, feelings, and sensations, which can reduce stress and improve emotional regulation.

2. Benefits of Mindfulness: Practicing mindfulness can help individuals with PTSD by reducing symptoms of anxiety and depression, improving concentration, and enhancing emotional resilience. It also promotes relaxation and helps individuals manage triggers and flashbacks.

3. Mindfulness Practices: There are several mindfulness practices that individuals can incorporate into their daily routine:
   - Breathing Exercises: Focusing on the breath can help calm the mind and reduce anxiety. Techniques such as deep breathing or counting breaths can be particularly effective.
   - Body Scan Meditation: This practice involves paying

attention to different parts of the body, noticing any tension or discomfort, and allowing these sensations to pass without judgment.

- Mindful Walking: Walking slowly and mindfully, paying attention to each step and the sensations in the body, can be a grounding practice.

- Mindful Eating: Eating slowly and savoring each bite, paying attention to the taste, texture, and smell of the food, can enhance mindfulness and enjoyment.

4. Meditation Techniques: Meditation can be a powerful tool for managing PTSD symptoms. Techniques include:

- Guided Meditation: Listening to a recorded meditation that guides the listener through relaxation and mindfulness exercises.

- Loving-Kindness Meditation: Focusing on cultivating feelings of compassion and kindness towards oneself and others.

- Visualization: Imagining a safe and peaceful place can help individuals feel more grounded and secure.

5. Creating a Routine: Establishing a regular mindfulness and meditation practice can enhance its benefits. Even dedicating a few minutes each day to these practices can make a significant difference.

After experiencing a traumatic event, Rachel struggled with anxiety and intrusive thoughts. She began practicing mindfulness and meditation as part of her recovery. Through daily breathing exercises and guided meditations, Rachel found a sense of calm and clarity. These practices helped her manage her anxiety and improved her overall well-being.

Mindfulness and meditation are accessible self-help strategies that can support recovery from PTSD. By incorporating these practices into their daily routine, individuals can enhance their emotional resilience and reduce the impact of trauma.

Exercise and Physical Health

Physical health and mental health are closely interconnected. Regular exercise can have a profound impact on managing PTSD symptoms and improving overall well-being. Engaging in physical activity can help reduce stress, improve mood, and enhance resilience.

Benefits of Exercise for PTSD:

1. Reducing Stress and Anxiety: Exercise helps reduce levels of the body's stress hormones, such as adrenaline and cortisol. It also stimulates the production of endorphins, which are natural mood lifters.

2. Improving Mood: Regular physical activity can help alleviate symptoms of depression and anxiety. Exercise releases neurotransmitters such as serotonin and dopamine, which are associated with improved mood and emotional well-being.

3. Enhancing Sleep: Exercise can improve sleep quality, which is often disrupted in individuals with PTSD. Better sleep can lead to improved concentration, mood, and overall health.

4. Boosting Self-Esteem: Regular physical activity can enhance self-esteem and body image. Achieving fitness goals, no matter how small, can provide a sense of accomplishment and confidence.

5. Providing a Distraction: Exercise can serve as a healthy distraction from intrusive thoughts and memories associated with PTSD. Engaging in physical activity can provide a break from the cycle of rumination and negative thinking.

Types of Exercise Beneficial for PTSD:

1. Aerobic Exercise: Activities such as running, swimming, cycling, and dancing can increase heart rate and release endorphins. These activities are particularly effective in

reducing anxiety and improving mood.

2. Strength Training: Weightlifting and resistance training can improve physical strength and body composition. Strength training can also enhance mental toughness and resilience.

3. Yoga: Yoga combines physical movement with mindfulness and breath control. It can improve flexibility, strength, and relaxation, making it an excellent practice for managing PTSD symptoms.

4. Martial Arts: Practices such as Tai Chi and martial arts can provide a structured way to release physical tension and build mental focus and discipline.

5. Outdoor Activities: Activities such as hiking, gardening, or playing sports can provide the benefits of exercise while also offering exposure to nature. Being in nature has additional calming and restorative effects.

Creating a Sustainable Exercise Routine:

1. Start Small: Begin with small, achievable goals and gradually increase the intensity and duration of the exercise. This can help build consistency and prevent burnout.

2. Find Enjoyable Activities: Choose activities that are enjoyable and align with personal interests. This increases the likelihood of maintaining a regular exercise routine.

3. Set Realistic Goals: Setting realistic and attainable goals can provide motivation and a sense of accomplishment. Celebrating small victories can boost confidence and commitment.

4. Incorporate Variety: Mixing different types of exercise can prevent boredom and work different muscle groups. Variety can also keep the exercise routine interesting and engaging.

After being diagnosed with PTSD, John found it difficult

to manage his anxiety and intrusive thoughts. His therapist recommended incorporating regular exercise into his routine. John started with daily walks in his neighborhood, gradually increasing the distance and pace. He then began attending a local yoga class, which helped him develop mindfulness and relaxation techniques. The combination of aerobic exercise and yoga significantly improved John's mood and reduced his anxiety, allowing him to feel more in control of his symptoms.

Regular exercise can be a powerful tool in managing PTSD and supporting overall mental health. By finding enjoyable and sustainable activities, individuals can improve their physical and emotional well-being.

Nutrition and Its Impact on Mental Health

Nutrition plays a crucial role in supporting mental health and managing PTSD symptoms. A balanced diet can improve mood, enhance energy levels, and support overall well-being. Understanding the connection between nutrition and mental health can empower individuals to make healthier food choices.

The Impact of Nutrition on PTSD:

1. Mood Regulation: Certain nutrients, such as omega-3 fatty acids, vitamins, and minerals, play a significant role in regulating mood and brain function. A diet rich in these nutrients can help stabilize mood and reduce symptoms of anxiety and depression.

2. Energy Levels: Eating a balanced diet that includes a variety of nutrients can help maintain stable energy levels throughout the day. This can improve concentration, reduce fatigue, and enhance overall functioning.

3. Brain Health: The brain requires a constant supply of nutrients to function optimally. A diet that supports brain health can improve cognitive function, memory, and emotional regulation.

4. Inflammation Reduction: Chronic inflammation has been linked to various mental health conditions, including PTSD. A diet rich in anti-inflammatory foods, such as fruits, vegetables, and whole grains, can help reduce inflammation and support mental health.

Nutritional Guidelines for Managing PTSD:

1. Omega-3 Fatty Acids: Found in fatty fish, flaxseeds, chia seeds, and walnuts, omega-3 fatty acids are essential for brain health and can help reduce inflammation.

2. Antioxidants: Foods rich in antioxidants, such as berries, leafy greens, and nuts, can protect the brain from oxidative stress and support overall health.

3. B Vitamins: B vitamins, particularly B6, B12, and folate, play a crucial role in brain function and mood regulation. These vitamins can be found in foods such as eggs, dairy, leafy greens, and legumes.

4. Magnesium: Magnesium is known for its calming effects and can help reduce symptoms of anxiety. It is found in foods such as dark chocolate, nuts, seeds, and whole grains.

5. Probiotics: Gut health is closely linked to mental health. Probiotics, found in fermented foods like yogurt, kefir, sauerkraut, and kimchi, can support a healthy gut microbiome and improve mood.

6. Hydration: Staying hydrated is essential for overall health and cognitive function. Drinking enough water throughout the day can help maintain energy levels and support mental clarity.

Creating a Balanced Meal Plan:

1. Incorporate Variety: Include a wide range of foods in your diet to ensure you are getting a variety of nutrients. Aim for colorful plates with different types of fruits and vegetables.

2. Plan Ahead: Planning meals and snacks ahead of time can help maintain a balanced diet and prevent reliance on unhealthy convenience foods.

3. Moderation: Practice moderation and avoid excessive consumption of processed foods, sugary snacks, and caffeine. These can negatively impact mood and energy levels.

4. Mindful Eating: Pay attention to hunger and fullness cues, and practice mindful eating. This involves savoring each bite and eating without distractions, which can improve digestion and satisfaction.

After being diagnosed with PTSD, Sarah noticed that her diet was affecting her mood and energy levels. She began working with a nutritionist to develop a balanced meal plan that included nutrient-dense foods. By incorporating more omega-3 fatty acids, antioxidants, and probiotics into her diet, Sarah experienced significant improvements in her mood and overall well-being. Nutrition became a key component of her self-help strategy, supporting her recovery journey.

Nutrition is a powerful tool in managing PTSD and supporting mental health. By making informed food choices and maintaining a balanced diet, individuals can enhance their emotional resilience and overall quality of life.

Journaling and Expressive Writing

Journaling and expressive writing are powerful self-help strategies that can support emotional healing and personal growth. These practices allow individuals to process their thoughts and feelings, gain insights into their experiences, and develop a greater sense of self-awareness.

Benefits of Journaling and Expressive Writing:

1. Emotional Release: Writing about thoughts and emotions can provide a healthy outlet for releasing pent-up feelings. This can

reduce stress and promote emotional well-being.

2. Clarifying Thoughts: Journaling helps individuals organize and make sense of their thoughts. It can bring clarity to complex emotions and situations, making it easier to understand and address them.

3. Processing Trauma: Writing about traumatic experiences can help individuals process and integrate these events into their life narrative. This can reduce the emotional intensity of the trauma and promote healing.

4. Identifying Patterns: Regular journaling can reveal patterns in thoughts, behaviors, and emotions. Recognizing these patterns can lead to greater self-awareness and more effective coping strategies.

5. Setting Goals: Journaling can be a valuable tool for setting and tracking personal goals. Writing about goals and progress can provide motivation and a sense of accomplishment.

Types of Journaling and Expressive Writing:

1. Free Writing: This involves writing continuously for a set period without worrying about grammar, spelling, or structure. Free writing allows for a stream-of-consciousness flow that can uncover hidden thoughts and feelings.

2. Prompt-Based Writing: Using prompts or questions as a starting point can help focus the writing and explore specific topics. Prompts can be related to emotions, experiences, or personal growth.

3. Gratitude Journaling: Writing about things one is grateful for can shift focus to positive aspects of life. This practice can improve mood and foster a sense of appreciation.

4. Reflective Journaling: Reflecting on daily experiences, challenges, and achievements can provide insights and promote personal growth. This type of journaling encourages self-

reflection and learning.

5. Creative Writing: Using creative writing techniques, such as poetry or storytelling, can provide a unique and expressive way to explore emotions and experiences.

Tips for Effective Journaling:

1. Find a Comfortable Space: Choose a quiet and comfortable space where you can write without interruptions. Creating a dedicated journaling environment can enhance the experience.

2. Be Honest: Write honestly and openly about your thoughts and feelings. Allow yourself to express emotions without judgment or censorship.

3. Set a Regular Schedule: Establishing a regular journaling routine can make the practice more effective. Even dedicating a few minutes each day to writing can make a significant difference.

4. Use Prompts: If you're unsure where to start, use writing prompts to guide your journaling. Prompts can provide inspiration and direction for your writing.

5. Review and Reflect: Periodically review your journal entries to reflect on your progress and gain insights. This can help track personal growth and identify areas for further exploration.

After experiencing a traumatic event, Emily struggled to process her emotions. She began keeping a journal to document her thoughts and feelings. Through regular journaling, Emily found a safe space to express her emotions and make sense of her experiences. The practice helped her identify patterns in her thoughts and develop healthier coping strategies. Over time, journaling became an essential part of Emily's healing process, providing clarity and emotional release.

Journaling and expressive writing are powerful tools for managing PTSD and supporting emotional well-being. By incorporating these practices into their routine, individuals can gain valuable insights, process their emotions, and promote personal growth.

The Power of Self-Help

David had always been an active and energetic person, but after surviving a serious car accident, he found himself struggling with severe anxiety and depression. His once vibrant life was overshadowed by fear and intrusive memories of the accident. Determined to reclaim his life, David decided to explore self-help strategies in addition to his professional treatment.

David began by incorporating mindfulness and meditation into his daily routine. He started with simple breathing exercises and gradually explored guided meditations. These practices helped him find a sense of calm and presence, reducing his anxiety and improving his ability to manage stress.

In addition to mindfulness, David made exercise a regular part of his life. He started with short walks around his neighborhood and gradually built up to jogging and strength training. The physical activity not only improved his mood but also provided a healthy outlet for his pent-up energy and tension.

David also paid close attention to his diet, ensuring that he included nutrient-dense foods that supported his mental and physical health. He worked with a nutritionist to develop a balanced meal plan rich in omega-3 fatty acids, antioxidants, and probiotics. This dietary change had a noticeable impact on his energy levels and overall well-being.

Journaling became another crucial aspect of David's self-help strategy. He dedicated time each evening to write about his thoughts and feelings. This practice helped him process his emotions, gain clarity, and track his progress. Through journaling, David discovered patterns in his behavior and developed effective coping strategies.

As David integrated these self-help strategies into his life, he began to notice significant improvements in his symptoms. His anxiety and depression became more manageable, and he regained a sense of control over his life. The combination of professional treatment and self-help practices provided a holistic approach to his recovery.

David's story is a testament to the power of self-help strategies in managing PTSD. By taking an active role in his recovery and exploring various approaches, David was able to build a comprehensive support system that addressed both his mind and body. His journey highlights the importance of persistence, self-awareness, and the willingness to try new things.

Self-help strategies can be a valuable addition to professional treatment for PTSD. By incorporating practices such as mindfulness, exercise, nutrition, and journaling, individuals can enhance their emotional resilience and overall quality of life. David's experience demonstrates that with the right tools and support, it is possible to overcome adversity and thrive.

CHAPTER 6: BUILDING A SUPPORT NETWORK

A strong support network is crucial for individuals dealing with PTSD. Supportive relationships provide emotional comfort, practical assistance, and a sense of belonging, all of which are vital for recovery and well-being.

The Importance of a Support Network:

1. Emotional Support: A support network offers a safe space for individuals to express their feelings and share their experiences without fear of judgment. This emotional support can alleviate feelings of isolation and loneliness.

2. Practical Assistance: Supportive relationships can provide practical help with daily tasks and responsibilities, reducing the stress and burden on the individual. This assistance can include help with household chores, childcare, or transportation.

3. Encouragement and Motivation: A support network can offer encouragement and motivation during challenging times. Positive reinforcement from loved ones can boost morale and inspire individuals to stay committed to their recovery goals.

4. Perspective and Insight: Friends, family, and support groups can offer different perspectives and insights that may help individuals understand their experiences and find new coping

strategies.

5. Sense of Belonging: Being part of a supportive community fosters a sense of belonging and connection. This can counteract the feelings of alienation and detachment often associated with PTSD.

After experiencing a traumatic event, Laura felt overwhelmed and isolated. She withdrew from her friends and family, believing that they wouldn't understand her struggles. However, when she finally opened up to her sister, she was met with compassion and understanding. Her sister became a vital source of emotional support, helping Laura navigate her recovery journey. This connection reminded Laura that she was not alone and that she had people who cared about her well-being.

Building a strong support network can make a significant difference in the recovery process. By reaching out and fostering supportive relationships, individuals can find the strength and resilience needed to heal.

Finding and Maintaining Supportive Relationships

Building and maintaining supportive relationships is essential for individuals with PTSD. These relationships can provide the foundation for emotional and practical support, aiding in the recovery process.

Finding Supportive Relationships:

1. Reconnecting with Loved Ones: Reaching out to family and friends can help re-establish connections and build a support network. Sharing experiences and feelings with trusted loved ones can strengthen bonds and provide much-needed support.

2. Joining Support Groups: Support groups offer a community of individuals who have faced similar challenges. These groups can provide a safe space for sharing experiences and receiving

support from others who understand.

3. Seeking Professional Help: Therapists, counselors, and mental health professionals can be an important part of a support network. They offer expert guidance and support tailored to the individual's needs.

4. Participating in Community Activities: Engaging in community activities, such as volunteering or joining clubs, can help individuals build new connections and expand their support network.

5. Online Communities: Online support groups and forums can provide a platform for individuals to connect with others who have similar experiences. These virtual communities offer flexibility and accessibility for those who may find it difficult to attend in-person meetings.

Maintaining Supportive Relationships:

1. Open Communication: Maintaining open and honest communication with loved ones is crucial. Sharing thoughts, feelings, and needs can help foster understanding and strengthen relationships.

2. Setting Boundaries: Establishing healthy boundaries is important in maintaining supportive relationships. This includes communicating limits and respecting each other's space and needs.

3. Showing Appreciation: Expressing gratitude and appreciation for the support received can strengthen relationships and encourage continued support.

4. Offering Support in Return: Being supportive to others can create a reciprocal relationship. Offering a listening ear or helping with tasks can strengthen the bond and build mutual support.

5. Staying Connected: Regularly staying in touch with loved

ones and support groups can help maintain the connection and ensure ongoing support. This can be through phone calls, video chats, or in-person meetings.

After his diagnosis of PTSD, Michael found it challenging to maintain his relationships. He often felt misunderstood and disconnected from others. However, by joining a local support group, he found a community of individuals who shared similar experiences. Through open communication and mutual support, Michael developed meaningful connections that provided him with the strength and encouragement he needed to continue his recovery journey.

Building and maintaining supportive relationships requires effort and commitment, but the rewards are invaluable. A strong support network can provide the foundation for healing and resilience.

The Role of Family and Friends

Family and friends play a vital role in supporting individuals with PTSD. Their understanding, patience, and support can make a significant difference in the recovery process. Here are some ways family and friends can offer support:

Supporting a Loved One with PTSD:

1. Educate Yourself: Understanding PTSD and its symptoms can help family and friends provide informed and compassionate support. Learning about the condition can also reduce misunderstandings and misconceptions.

2. Listen Without Judgment: Offering a listening ear without judgment is one of the most powerful ways to support someone with PTSD. Allowing them to share their experiences and feelings can provide emotional relief and validation.

3. Encourage Professional Help: Encouraging the individual to seek professional help and supporting them in accessing

treatment can be crucial. This may involve helping them find a therapist, attending appointments with them, or providing transportation.

4. Be Patient: Recovery from PTSD can be a long and challenging journey. Patience is essential, as progress may be slow, and setbacks may occur. Offering consistent support and understanding can help the individual feel more secure.

5. Respect Boundaries: Respecting the individual's boundaries and giving them space when needed is important. Avoid pushing them to talk about their trauma if they are not ready.

6. Offer Practical Support: Providing practical assistance with daily tasks can reduce stress and allow the individual to focus on their recovery. This can include helping with household chores, running errands, or providing childcare.

7. Create a Safe Environment: Creating a safe and supportive environment at home can help the individual feel more secure. This includes minimizing potential triggers and ensuring a calm and comforting atmosphere.

8. Encourage Healthy Habits: Encouraging healthy habits, such as regular exercise, a balanced diet, and mindfulness practices, can support overall well-being and recovery.

After witnessing a traumatic event at work, Sam struggled with severe PTSD. His wife, Emily, became his primary support system. She educated herself about PTSD, attended therapy sessions with Sam, and provided unwavering emotional support. Emily's patience and understanding helped Sam feel safe and encouraged him to continue his treatment. Together, they navigated the challenges of recovery, and Sam found strength in the support of his family.

Family and friends can be a lifeline for individuals with PTSD. Their love, understanding, and support can provide the foundation for healing and recovery.

Joining Support Groups

Support groups offer a valuable resource for individuals with PTSD. These groups provide a safe space for sharing experiences, receiving support, and learning from others who have faced similar challenges.

Benefits of Joining Support Groups:

1. Shared Experiences: Support groups allow individuals to connect with others who have experienced similar traumas. Sharing stories and hearing others' experiences can provide validation and reduce feelings of isolation.

2. Emotional Support: Being part of a support group offers a sense of community and belonging. Members can offer emotional support, encouragement, and understanding, which can be incredibly healing.

3. Learning and Insight: Support groups provide an opportunity to learn from others' coping strategies and experiences. Members can share practical advice and insights that can be applied to their own recovery journey.

4. Safe Space: Support groups offer a safe and non-judgmental environment where individuals can express their thoughts and feelings freely. This can be particularly beneficial for those who may feel hesitant to open up in other settings.

5. Accountability: Regularly attending support group meetings can provide a sense of accountability and motivation to stay committed to the recovery process. Knowing that others are on a similar journey can inspire individuals to keep working towards their goals.

Finding the Right Support Group:

1. Research Options: There are various types of support groups available, including those specific to PTSD, trauma, or certain

types of experiences (e.g., military veterans, survivors of abuse). Researching options can help find a group that aligns with individual needs.

2. Consider Format: Support groups can be in-person or online. In-person groups offer face-to-face interaction, while online groups provide flexibility and accessibility for those who may find it difficult to attend meetings in person.

3. Evaluate Fit: It may take some time to find the right support group. Attending a few different groups can help determine which one feels like the best fit in terms of dynamics, support, and comfort level.

4. Ask for Recommendations: Mental health professionals, therapists, and community organizations can provide recommendations for reputable support groups. They may also have information about local resources and meeting times.

5. Check Credentials: Ensuring that the support group is facilitated by a qualified professional or experienced peer leader can enhance the quality and safety of the group.

After struggling with PTSD for years, Sarah decided to join a local support group for trauma survivors. At first, she was hesitant to share her story, but as she listened to others, she realized she was not alone. The support and understanding she received from the group members provided her with a sense of comfort and belonging. Through the support group, Sarah gained new coping strategies and made meaningful connections that supported her recovery journey.

Joining a support group can be a transformative experience for individuals with PTSD. The sense of community, shared experiences, and emotional support can provide invaluable assistance on the path to healing.

The Strength in Community

After experiencing a traumatic event, David found himself struggling with severe PTSD. His symptoms included flashbacks, anxiety, and a

pervasive sense of fear. Despite seeking professional help, David felt isolated and disconnected from those around him. He knew he needed additional support and decided to join a support group for trauma survivors.

At his first support group meeting, David was nervous and unsure of what to expect. However, as he listened to others share their stories, he felt a sense of relief. He realized that he was not alone in his struggles and that others had faced similar challenges. The support group provided a safe space where he could express his feelings without fear of judgment.

Over time, David began to share his own experiences with the group. The understanding and empathy he received from the other members helped him feel validated and supported. He also learned new coping strategies from the group members, which he incorporated into his daily routine.

One of the most significant benefits David found in the support group was the sense of community. He formed meaningful connections with others who understood his journey. These relationships provided him with emotional support, encouragement, and a sense of belonging. The group became a source of strength for David, helping him navigate the challenges of PTSD.

As David continued to attend the support group, he noticed significant improvements in his symptoms. He felt more confident and less isolated. The support and understanding he received from the group members empowered him to continue his recovery journey.

David's story highlights the power of community and the

importance of a strong support network. The connections he made in the support group provided him with the strength and resilience he needed to heal. His experience demonstrates that with the right support, it is possible to overcome adversity and find hope and healing.

Building a support network and joining support groups can be invaluable for individuals with PTSD. The sense of community, shared experiences, and emotional support can provide the foundation for healing and recovery.

CHAPTER 7: MINDFULNESS AND MEDITATION

Mindfulness and meditation are powerful tools for managing PTSD and promoting overall mental health. These practices help individuals become more aware of their thoughts and emotions, fostering a sense of calm and resilience.

Introduction to Mindfulness:

1. Definition of Mindfulness: Mindfulness involves paying attention to the present moment with an attitude of openness and non-judgment. It encourages individuals to observe their thoughts, feelings, and sensations without getting caught up in them.

2. Benefits of Mindfulness: Practicing mindfulness can reduce symptoms of anxiety and depression, improve concentration, and enhance emotional regulation. It helps individuals develop a greater sense of self-awareness and acceptance.

3. Mindfulness and PTSD: For individuals with PTSD, mindfulness can provide a way to manage intrusive thoughts and emotions. By staying present and observing their experiences without judgment, individuals can reduce the power of traumatic memories and find greater peace.

4. Basic Mindfulness Practices: There are several simple

mindfulness practices that individuals can incorporate into their daily lives:

- Mindful Breathing: Focusing on the breath and observing its natural rhythm can help calm the mind and reduce anxiety.

- Body Scan: Paying attention to different parts of the body and noticing sensations without judgment can promote relaxation and awareness.

- Mindful Walking: Walking slowly and mindfully, paying attention to each step and the sensations in the body, can be a grounding practice.

- Mindful Eating: Eating slowly and savoring each bite, paying attention to the taste, texture, and smell of the food, can enhance mindfulness and enjoyment.

After experiencing a traumatic event, Maria struggled with constant anxiety and intrusive thoughts. She began practicing mindfulness as part of her recovery. Through daily mindful breathing exercises and body scans, Maria found a sense of calm and clarity. These practices helped her manage her anxiety and improved her overall well-being.

Mindfulness is a powerful and accessible practice that can support recovery from PTSD. By incorporating mindfulness into their daily routine, individuals can enhance their emotional resilience and reduce the impact of trauma.

Meditation Techniques for PTSD

Meditation is a practice that involves focusing the mind and eliminating distractions to achieve a state of relaxation and clarity. Different meditation techniques can be particularly beneficial for managing PTSD symptoms.

Types of Meditation Techniques:

1. Guided Meditation: Guided meditation involves listening to a recorded meditation that leads the listener through a series of relaxation and mindfulness exercises. This type of meditation

can help individuals focus their mind and achieve a state of calm.

2. Loving-Kindness Meditation: Also known as Metta meditation, this practice involves focusing on cultivating feelings of compassion and kindness towards oneself and others. It can help reduce feelings of anger and resentment and promote emotional healing.

3. Body Scan Meditation: This technique involves mentally scanning the body from head to toe, paying attention to any areas of tension or discomfort. By observing these sensations without judgment, individuals can promote relaxation and awareness.

4. Visualization: Visualization involves imagining a safe and peaceful place, such as a beach or forest. This practice can help individuals feel more grounded and secure, reducing feelings of anxiety and fear.

5. Mantra Meditation: Mantra meditation involves repeating a word or phrase, known as a mantra, to help focus the mind and achieve a state of relaxation. The repetition of the mantra can create a sense of calm and reduce intrusive thoughts.

How to Practice Meditation:

1. Find a Quiet Space: Choose a quiet and comfortable space where you can meditate without distractions. This could be a dedicated meditation room or a quiet corner of your home.

2. Set a Time Limit: Start with short meditation sessions, such as 5-10 minutes, and gradually increase the duration as you become more comfortable with the practice.

3. Focus on Your Breath: Begin by focusing on your breath, observing the natural rhythm of inhalation and exhalation. If your mind starts to wander, gently bring your focus back to your breath.

4. Use Guided Meditations: If you are new to meditation, using guided meditations can be helpful. There are many apps and online resources that offer guided meditations specifically designed for PTSD and anxiety.

5. Be Patient and Consistent: Meditation is a skill that takes time to develop. Be patient with yourself and practice regularly to experience the full benefits.

After being diagnosed with PTSD, John found it difficult to manage his anxiety and intrusive thoughts. His therapist recommended meditation as part of his treatment plan. John started with guided meditations and gradually explored different techniques, such as body scan and loving-kindness meditation. These practices helped him achieve a sense of calm and reduced his anxiety. Over time, meditation became an essential part of John's daily routine, supporting his recovery and overall well-being.

Meditation offers a variety of techniques that can help individuals manage PTSD symptoms and promote emotional healing. By incorporating these practices into their daily routine, individuals can find greater peace and resilience.

Guided Imagery and Visualization

Guided imagery and visualization are powerful techniques that involve using the imagination to create calming and positive mental images. These practices can help individuals with PTSD reduce anxiety, manage stress, and promote relaxation.

Understanding Guided Imagery and Visualization:

1. Guided Imagery: Guided imagery involves following a script or recording that leads the individual through a series of mental images designed to promote relaxation and healing. This practice can help individuals focus their mind and achieve a

state of calm.

2. Visualization: Visualization involves imagining a peaceful and safe place or situation. By focusing on positive and calming images, individuals can reduce anxiety and enhance their sense of well-being.

Benefits of Guided Imagery and Visualization:

1. Reducing Anxiety: Guided imagery and visualization can help reduce symptoms of anxiety by promoting relaxation and reducing the focus on negative thoughts.

2. Managing Stress: These practices provide a mental escape from stressors, allowing individuals to feel more relaxed and grounded.

3. Enhancing Emotional Regulation: By focusing on positive and calming images, individuals can improve their emotional regulation and reduce the intensity of negative emotions.

4. Promoting Healing: Guided imagery and visualization can support the healing process by creating a sense of safety and security. These practices can help individuals feel more in control of their mental and emotional state.

How to Practice Guided Imagery and Visualization:

1. Find a Comfortable Position: Choose a comfortable position, either sitting or lying down, where you can relax and focus without distractions.

2. Use a Script or Recording: Guided imagery scripts and recordings are widely available online and through meditation apps. Choose one that resonates with you and follow along with the instructions.

3. Focus on Your Breath: Begin by taking a few deep breaths to help calm your mind and body. Focus on the natural rhythm of your breath.

4. Create a Mental Image: Visualize a peaceful and safe place, such as a beach, forest, or garden. Use all your senses to make the image as vivid as possible. Imagine the sights, sounds, smells, and sensations of your chosen place.

5. Stay Present: Allow yourself to fully immerse in the mental image. If your mind starts to wander, gently bring your focus back to the visualization.

6. Practice Regularly: Consistent practice can enhance the benefits of guided imagery and visualization. Aim to incorporate these techniques into your daily routine.

After experiencing a traumatic event, Emma struggled with severe anxiety and panic attacks. Her therapist introduced her to guided imagery as a way to manage her symptoms. Emma began using guided imagery recordings to visualize a peaceful beach, where she felt safe and calm. Over time, this practice helped her reduce her anxiety and regain a sense of control. Guided imagery became a valuable tool in Emma's recovery journey, providing her with a mental escape from her stressors.

Guided imagery and visualization are powerful techniques that can help individuals with PTSD manage their symptoms and promote relaxation. By incorporating these practices into their daily routine, individuals can enhance their emotional resilience and overall well-being.

Daily Mindfulness Practices

Incorporating mindfulness into daily life can provide ongoing support for managing PTSD symptoms and promoting overall mental health. These practices help individuals stay present, reduce stress, and enhance emotional regulation.

1. Mindful Breathing: Take a few minutes each day to focus on your breath. Observe the natural rhythm of inhalation and exhalation. If your mind starts to wander, gently bring your

focus back to your breath. This practice can be done anytime and anywhere, providing a quick and effective way to reduce stress.

2. Mindful Walking: Engage in mindful walking by paying attention to each step and the sensations in your body. Notice the feeling of your feet touching the ground, the movement of your legs, and the rhythm of your breath. This practice can be incorporated into your daily routine, whether walking in nature or around your home.

3. Mindful Eating: Practice mindful eating by savoring each bite of your food. Pay attention to the taste, texture, and smell of the food. Eat slowly and without distractions, such as TV or phones. This practice can enhance your enjoyment of food and promote better digestion.

4. Body Scan: Perform a body scan by mentally scanning your body from head to toe. Pay attention to any areas of tension or discomfort and observe these sensations without judgment. This practice can promote relaxation and awareness of your body's needs.

5. Mindful Listening: Practice mindful listening by giving your full attention to the sounds around you. Whether it's the sound of birds, music, or a conversation, focus on the act of listening without judgment or distraction. This practice can enhance your connection with your environment and improve your listening skills.

6. Gratitude Practice: Take a few minutes each day to reflect on things youare grateful for. Write them down in a gratitude journal or simply take a moment to acknowledge them. This practice can shift your focus to positive aspects of your life and improve your overall mood.

Tips for Incorporating Mindfulness into Daily Life:

1. Start Small: Begin with short mindfulness practices

and gradually increase the duration as you become more comfortable. Even a few minutes of mindfulness each day can make a significant difference.

2. Be Consistent: Establish a regular mindfulness routine by setting aside specific times each day for practice. Consistency can enhance the benefits and make mindfulness a natural part of your life.

3. Be Present: Focus on being fully present in whatever you are doing. Whether it's washing dishes, driving, or having a conversation, bring your attention to the present moment and observe your thoughts and feelings without judgment.

4. Use Reminders: Set reminders on your phone or place visual cues around your home to prompt you to practice mindfulness. These reminders can help you stay on track and incorporate mindfulness into your daily routine.

5. Practice Self-Compassion: Approach your mindfulness practice with self-compassion and patience. It's normal for your mind to wander or for some days to be more challenging than others. Be kind to yourself and continue practicing without judgment.

After being diagnosed with PTSD, Alex struggled with constant anxiety and intrusive thoughts. He began incorporating daily mindfulness practices into his routine, starting with mindful breathing and body scans. Over time, he added mindful walking and gratitude practice to his daily activities. These practices helped Alex stay present and manage his anxiety more effectively. Mindfulness became a cornerstone of his recovery, providing him with a sense of calm and resilience.

Daily mindfulness practices offer a simple and effective way to manage PTSD symptoms and promote overall well-being. By incorporating these practices into their routine, individuals can enhance their emotional resilience and find greater peace in everyday life.

Finding Peace in Stillness

Samantha had always been a high-achieving individual, constantly on the go and juggling multiple responsibilities. However, after surviving a traumatic event, she found herself struggling with severe anxiety and intrusive thoughts. Her once busy and fulfilling life felt overwhelming and out of control.

Desperate for relief, Samantha decided to explore mindfulness and meditation as part of her recovery. She started with simple mindfulness practices, such as mindful breathing and body scans. At first, it was challenging for her to sit still and focus her mind. However, she persisted and gradually began to notice small changes.

Samantha then introduced guided imagery and visualization into her routine. She found solace in imagining peaceful and safe places, such as a serene beach or a quiet forest. These practices provided her with a mental escape from her anxiety and helped her feel more grounded.

As she became more comfortable with mindfulness, Samantha added daily meditation sessions to her routine. She explored different meditation techniques, such as loving-kindness meditation and mantra meditation. These practices helped her cultivate feelings of compassion and kindness towards herself, which was crucial for her healing process.

Over time, Samantha noticed significant improvements in her symptoms. Her anxiety became more manageable, and she experienced fewer intrusive thoughts. The mindfulness and meditation practices provided her with tools to stay present and calm, even in stressful situations.

Samantha's journey with mindfulness and meditation taught her the importance of stillness and self-awareness. These practices became an essential part of her daily life, supporting her recovery and overall well-being. Samantha found peace in the stillness, learning to embrace the present moment and let go of her fears.

Her story is a testament to the power of mindfulness and meditation in managing PTSD and promoting emotional resilience. By incorporating these practices into her routine, Samantha was able to find a sense of calm and control, ultimately transforming her life.

Finding peace in stillness is possible through mindfulness and meditation. These practices offer a powerful and accessible way to manage PTSD symptoms and enhance emotional well-being. Samantha's experience demonstrates that with persistence and dedication, it is possible to overcome adversity and find greater peace and resilience.

CHAPTER 8: EXERCISE AND PHYSICAL HEALTH

Exercise and physical health play a crucial role in managing PTSD and promoting overall mental well-being. The connection between physical activity and mental health is well-documented, highlighting the importance of incorporating regular exercise into the recovery process.

The Connection Between Physical and Mental Health:

1. Stress Reduction: Exercise helps reduce levels of stress hormones, such as cortisol and adrenaline, while simultaneously increasing the production of endorphins, which are natural mood elevators. This physiological response can lead to a reduction in stress and anxiety.

2. Improved Mood: Regular physical activity is associated with improved mood and reduced symptoms of depression. Exercise stimulates the release of neurotransmitters, such as serotonin and dopamine, which are linked to feelings of happiness and well-being.

3. Enhanced Cognitive Function: Exercise has been shown to improve cognitive function, including memory, attention, and executive function. This can be particularly beneficial for individuals with PTSD, who may experience difficulties with concentration and memory.

4. Better Sleep: Regular physical activity can improve sleep quality and reduce symptoms of insomnia, which are common in individuals with PTSD. Better sleep contributes to overall mental and physical health.

5. Increased Resilience: Engaging in regular exercise can enhance resilience by improving physical strength and endurance, which can translate into greater mental toughness and the ability to cope with stress.

6. Social Interaction: Many forms of exercise, such as team sports or group fitness classes, provide opportunities for social interaction and support. Building social connections through physical activity can help reduce feelings of isolation and loneliness.

After being diagnosed with PTSD, Jake found it challenging to manage his anxiety and intrusive thoughts. His therapist recommended incorporating regular exercise into his routine. Jake started with daily walks and gradually included running and strength training. The physical activity helped him reduce stress, improve his mood, and feel more in control of his symptoms. Exercise became a crucial part of Jake's recovery, supporting his mental and physical well-being.

Exercise offers a range of benefits for individuals with PTSD, helping to reduce symptoms and promote overall health. By understanding the connection between physical and mental health, individuals can leverage exercise as a powerful tool in their recovery journey.

Types of Exercise Beneficial for PTSD

Different types of exercise can offer unique benefits for individuals with PTSD. Finding the right type of physical activity can enhance enjoyment and effectiveness in managing symptoms.

Types of Exercise Beneficial for PTSD:

1. Aerobic Exercise: Activities such as running, swimming, cycling, and dancing increase heart rate and stimulate the release of endorphins. Aerobic exercise is particularly effective in reducing anxiety and depression.

2. Strength Training: Weightlifting and resistance training can improve physical strength and body composition. Strength training can also boost self-esteem and provide a sense of accomplishment.

3. Yoga: Yoga combines physical movement with mindfulness and breath control. It can improve flexibility, strength, and relaxation, making it an excellent practice for managing PTSD symptoms. Yoga also promotes mindfulness, which can help individuals stay present and reduce the impact of traumatic memories.

4. Martial Arts: Practices such as Tai Chi, Judo, and Karate provide a structured way to release physical tension and build mental focus and discipline. Martial arts can also enhance self-confidence and provide a sense of control.

5. Outdoor Activities: Engaging in outdoor activities such as hiking, gardening, or kayaking can provide the benefits of exercise while also offering exposure to nature. Being in nature has additional calming and restorative effects.

6. Dance Therapy: Dance therapy involves using movement to express emotions and release physical tension. It can be a creative and enjoyable way to process trauma and improve mental health.

How to Choose the Right Type of Exercise:

1. Personal Preferences: Choose activities that you enjoy and find engaging. This increases the likelihood of maintaining a regular exercise routine.

2. Physical Abilities: Consider your current physical fitness level and any limitations. Start with activities that are appropriate for your abilities and gradually increase the intensity.

3. Availability: Choose activities that are easily accessible and fit into your schedule. This can include at-home workouts, local fitness classes, or outdoor activities.

4. Variety: Incorporate a variety of exercises to work different muscle groups and prevent boredom. Mixing different types of physical activity can keep the exercise routine interesting and effective.

After experiencing a traumatic event, Sarah struggled with severe anxiety and depression. She decided to explore different types of exercise to find what worked best for her. Sarah started with yoga and found the combination of movement and mindfulness incredibly beneficial. She then added swimming and hiking to her routine, enjoying the physical activity and the time spent in nature. The variety of exercises helped Sarah manage her symptoms and improve her overall well-being.

Finding the right type of exercise can make a significant difference in managing PTSD symptoms and promoting mental health. By exploring different activities, individuals can discover what works best for them and create a balanced and enjoyable exercise routine.

Creating a Sustainable Exercise Routine

Developing a sustainable exercise routine is key to maintaining the benefits of physical activity for managing PTSD. Consistency is crucial for long-term success, and creating a routine that fits into your lifestyle can help ensure ongoing engagement.

Steps to Creating a Sustainable Exercise Routine:

1. Set Realistic Goals: Start with small, achievable goals that can

be gradually increased over time. Setting realistic goals helps build confidence and provides a sense of accomplishment.

2. Make a Schedule: Plan your exercise sessions in advance and incorporate them into your daily or weekly schedule. Treat these sessions as important appointments that you are committed to keeping.

3. Choose Enjoyable Activities: Select exercises that you enjoy and look forward to doing. This increases the likelihood of sticking with the routine and makes exercise a positive experience.

4. Mix It Up: Incorporate a variety of exercises to work different muscle groups and prevent boredom. Combining aerobic activities, strength training, and flexibility exercises can create a balanced routine.

5. Find a Workout Buddy: Exercising with a friend or joining a fitness group can provide motivation and accountability. Social support can enhance the enjoyment of physical activity and help you stay committed.

6. Listen to Your Body: Pay attention to how your body feels during and after exercise. It's important to avoid overexertion and allow for rest and recovery. Adjust the intensity and duration of your workouts based on your physical condition.

7. Track Your Progress: Keeping a fitness journal or using a fitness app to track your workouts can help monitor your progress and stay motivated. Recording your achievements and challenges can provide valuable insights and encouragement.

8. Stay Flexible: Life can be unpredictable, and it's important to be flexible with your exercise routine. If you miss a workout, don't be discouraged. Simply adjust your schedule and get back on track as soon as possible.

After being diagnosed with PTSD, David knew that exercise could be beneficial for his recovery. He started by setting realistic goals, such as walking for 20 minutes three times a week. As he became more comfortable with his routine, he added strength training and yoga. David found a workout buddy who shared similar goals, and they motivated each other to stay committed. By tracking his progress and staying flexible, David created a sustainable exercise routine that supported his mental and physical health.

Creating a sustainable exercise routine involves setting realistic goals, choosing enjoyable activities, and staying flexible. By incorporating these strategies, individuals can maintain the benefits of physical activity and support their recovery from PTSD.

The Role of Outdoor Activities and Nature

Spending time in nature and engaging in outdoor activities can have a profound impact on mental health and well-being. Nature provides a calming and restorative environment that can help reduce stress and enhance emotional resilience.

Benefits of Outdoor Activities and Nature:

1. Reduced Stress: Being in nature has been shown to reduce levels of cortisol, the body's stress hormone. The natural environment promotes relaxation and can help alleviate feelings of stress and anxiety.

2. Improved Mood: Exposure to natural light and fresh air can improve mood and reduce symptoms of depression. Outdoor activities stimulate the production of serotonin and endorphins, which are associated with feelings of happiness and well-being.

3. Enhanced Cognitive Function: Spending time in nature can improve cognitive function, including attention, memory, and problem-solving skills. Nature provides a mentally restorative environment that can enhance focus and clarity.

4. Increased Physical Activity: Outdoor activities often involve

physical movement, such as hiking, biking, or gardening. These activities provide the benefits of exercise while also allowing individuals to connect with nature.

5. Greater Sense of Connection: Nature can foster a sense of connection and belonging. Being in natural settings can help individuals feel more grounded and connected to the world around them.

Types of Outdoor Activities Beneficial for PTSD:

1. Hiking: Hiking provides a great way to explore nature while engaging in physical activity. The rhythmic movement and natural surroundings can promote relaxation and reduce stress.

2. Gardening: Gardening offers a hands-on way to connect with nature and enjoy the benefits of physical activity. Tending to plants can be a meditative and rewarding experience.

3. Kayaking or Canoeing: Water-based activities like kayaking or canoeing provide a unique way to experience nature. The rhythmic motion of paddling and the calming effect of water can enhance relaxation.

4. Biking: Biking allows individuals to cover more ground and explore different natural areas. It combines physical activity with the benefits of being outdoors.

5. Nature Walks: Simple nature walks can be a relaxing and enjoyable way to spend time in nature. Walking at a leisurely pace allows individuals to fully appreciate the sights, sounds, and smells of the natural environment.

6. Camping: Camping provides an immersive experience in nature. Spending extended time outdoors can help individuals disconnect from daily stressors and reconnect with the natural world.

After experiencing a traumatic event, Emily struggled with severe anxiety and depression. She decided to spend more time outdoors as part of her recovery. Emily began with short nature walks and gradually explored hiking and kayaking. The time spent in nature provided her with a sense of calm and helped reduce her anxiety. The physical activity and connection to nature became a vital part of Emily's healing process.

Engaging in outdoor activities and spending time in nature can provide significant benefits for individuals with PTSD. The natural environment offers a calming and restorative setting that supports mental and physical well-being.

Healing Through Movement

After serving in the military, Tom returned home with severe PTSD. He experienced frequent flashbacks, anxiety, and a deep sense of isolation. Traditional therapies provided some relief, but Tom knew he needed something more to regain control of his life.

Tom decided to explore different types of exercise as part of his recovery. He started with simple activities, such as walking and stretching. These initial steps helped him build confidence and establish a routine. Encouraged by the positive effects, Tom gradually introduced more challenging activities, such as running and strength training.

Tom discovered that exercise provided a powerful outlet for his pent-up energy and emotions. Running became a form of moving meditation for him, allowing him to clear his mind and focus on the present moment. Strength training helped him feel physically strong and capable, which translated into greater mental resilience.

In addition to traditional exercise, Tom embraced outdoor activities. He found solace in hiking and kayaking, which allowed him to connect with nature and find peace in the natural environment. The combination of physical activity and the calming effect of nature provided a comprehensive approach to his recovery.

Tom also joined a local fitness group, where he met others who shared similar goals. The social support and camaraderie he found in the group helped reduce his feelings of isolation and provided additional motivation to stay committed to his exercise routine.

Through consistent exercise and outdoor activities, Tom noticed significant improvements in his symptoms. His anxiety became more manageable, and he experienced fewer flashbacks. The physical activity helped him sleep better and improved his overall mood. Exercise became a cornerstone of Tom's recovery, providing him with the tools to heal and rebuild his life.

Tom's story demonstrates the transformative power of exercise and physical activity in managing PTSD. By embracing movement and exploring different activities, Tom was able to find a sense of control and resilience. His journey highlights the importance of staying active and finding what works best for each individual.

Healing through movement is possible, and exercise can be a powerful tool in the recovery process. By incorporating regular physical activity into their routine, individuals with PTSD can enhance their mental and physical well-being and find a path to healing.

CHAPTER 9: NUTRITION AND MENTAL HEALTH

Nutrition plays a crucial role in supporting mental health and managing PTSD symptoms. A balanced diet can improve mood, enhance energy levels, and support overall well-being. Understanding the connection between nutrition and mental health can empower individuals to make healthier food choices.

The Impact of Diet on Mental Health:

1. Mood Regulation: Certain nutrients, such as omega-3 fatty acids, vitamins, and minerals, play a significant role in regulating mood and brain function. A diet rich in these nutrients can help stabilize mood and reduce symptoms of anxiety and depression.

2. Energy Levels: Eating a balanced diet that includes a variety of nutrients can help maintain stable energy levels throughout the day. This can improve concentration, reduce fatigue, and enhance overall functioning.

3. Brain Health: The brain requires a constant supply of nutrients to function optimally. A diet that supports brain health can improve cognitive function, memory, and emotional regulation.

4. Inflammation Reduction: Chronic inflammation has been

linked to various mental health conditions, including PTSD. A diet rich in anti-inflammatory foods, such as fruits, vegetables, and whole grains, can help reduce inflammation and support mental health.

5. Gut Health: The gut-brain connection is a critical aspect of mental health. A healthy gut microbiome can influence mood and behavior. Consuming probiotics and fibre-rich foods can support gut health and improve overall well-being.

After being diagnosed with PTSD, Sarah noticed that her diet was affecting her mood and energy levels. She began working with a nutritionist to develop a balanced meal plan that included nutrient-dense foods. By incorporating more omega-3 fatty acids, antioxidants, and probiotics into her diet, Sarah experienced significant improvements in her mood and overall well-being. Nutrition became a key component of her self-help strategy, supporting her recovery journey.

Understanding the impact of diet on mental health is the first step towards making positive dietary changes. By focusing on nutrient-rich foods, individuals can support their mental and physical health.

Nutritional Guidelines for Managing PTSD

Adopting a balanced and nutrient-rich diet can help manage PTSD symptoms and support overall mental health. Here are some key nutritional guidelines to consider:

1. Omega-3 Fatty Acids:
- Benefits: Omega-3 fatty acids are essential for brain health and can help reduce inflammation. They have been linked to improved mood and cognitive function.
- Sources: Fatty fish (such as salmon, mackerel, and sardines), flaxseeds, chia seeds, walnuts, and algae-based supplements.

2. Antioxidants:
- Benefits: Antioxidants protect the brain from oxidative stress

and support overall health. They can help reduce symptoms of anxiety and depression.
- Sources: Berries (such as blueberries, strawberries, and raspberries), dark leafy greens (such as spinach and kale), nuts, seeds, and dark chocolate.

3. B Vitamins:
- Benefits: B vitamins, particularly B6, B12, and folate, play a crucial role in brain function and mood regulation. They can help reduce symptoms of depression and improve cognitive function.
- Sources: Eggs, dairy products, leafy greens, legumes, and fortified cereals.

4. Magnesium:
- Benefits: Magnesium is known for its calming effects and can help reduce symptoms of anxiety and improve sleep quality.
- Sources: Dark chocolate, nuts, seeds, whole grains, and leafy greens.

5. Probiotics:
- Benefits: Probiotics support a healthy gut microbiome, which is closely linked to mental health. A healthy gut can influence mood and behavior.
- Sources: Yogurt, kefir, sauerkraut, kimchi, and other fermented foods.

6. Protein:
- Benefits: Protein provides the building blocks for neurotransmitters, which are essential for brain function and mood regulation.
- Sources: Lean meats, poultry, fish, eggs, dairy products, legumes, and nuts.

7. Complex Carbohydrates:
- Benefits: Complex carbohydrates provide a steady source of energy and can help stabilize blood sugar levels, reducing mood swings and fatigue.

- Sources: Whole grains, fruits, vegetables, and legumes.

8. Hydration:
- Benefits: Staying hydrated is essential for overall health and cognitive function. Dehydration can negatively impact mood and energy levels.
- Sources: Water, herbal teas, and water-rich foods (such as fruits and vegetables).

After experiencing a traumatic event, Mark struggled with severe anxiety and depression. He decided to focus on his diet to support his mental health. Mark incorporated more omega-3 fatty acids, antioxidants, and probiotics into his meals. He also ensured he stayed hydrated and included a variety of nutrient-rich foods in his diet. These changes had a significant positive impact on his mood and energy levels, supporting his recovery from PTSD.

Following these nutritional guidelines can help individuals with PTSD manage their symptoms and support overall mental health. By making informed food choices, individuals can enhance their well-being and resilience.

Supplements and Their Benefits

While a balanced diet should be the primary source of nutrients, supplements can provide additional support for managing PTSD symptoms. Here are some supplements that may be beneficial for mental health:

1. Omega-3 Fatty Acids:
- Benefits: Omega-3 supplements can help reduce inflammation and support brain health. They have been shown to improve mood and cognitive function.
- Forms: Fish oil supplements, algae-based supplements (for vegetarians and vegans).

2. Vitamin D:
- Benefits: Vitamin D plays a crucial role in brain function and

mood regulation. It can help reduce symptoms of depression and improve overall mental health.
- Forms: Vitamin D3 supplements, often available in liquid, capsule, or tablet form.

3. B Vitamins:
- Benefits: B vitamins, particularly B6, B12, and folate, are essential for brain function and mood regulation. They can help reduce symptoms of depression and improve cognitive function.
- Forms: B-complex supplements, individual B vitamin supplements.

4. Magnesium:
- Benefits: Magnesium supplements can help reduce symptoms of anxiety and improve sleep quality. Magnesium has calming effects and supports overall mental health.
- Forms: Magnesium citrate, magnesium glycinate, magnesium oxide.

5. Probiotics:
- Benefits: Probiotics support a healthy gut microbiome, which is closely linked to mental health. A healthy gut can influence mood and behavior.
- Forms: Probiotic capsules, probiotic powders, fermented foods.

6. Zinc:
- Benefits: Zinc is important for brain function and immune health. It can help reduce symptoms of depression and support overall well-being.
- Forms: Zinc citrate, zinc gluconate, zinc picolinate.

7. Adaptogens:
- Benefits: Adaptogens are herbs and natural substances that help the body adapt to stress. They can support mental resilience and reduce symptoms of anxiety.
- Forms: Ashwagandha, Rhodiola Rosea, holy basil, available in capsules, powders, and teas.

Considerations When Taking Supplements:
- Consult a Healthcare Provider: Before starting any new supplement, it is important to consult with a healthcare provider to ensure it is safe and appropriate for your individual needs.
- Quality and Dosage: Choose high-quality supplements from reputable brands. Follow the recommended dosage instructions and avoid taking excessive amounts.
- Monitor Effects: Pay attention to how your body responds to supplements and report any adverse effects to your healthcare provider.

After struggling with PTSD, Emily decided to explore supplements to support her mental health. She started with omega-3 fish oil supplements and a B-complex vitamin. Over time, she noticed improvements in her mood and cognitive function. Emily also added magnesium to help with her anxiety and sleep. The combination of these supplements, along with a balanced diet, provided her with additional support in managing her symptoms.

Supplements can offer valuable support for individuals with PTSD, but they should be used in conjunction with a balanced diet and under the guidance of a healthcare provider. By choosing the right supplements, individuals can enhance their mental and physical well-being.

Creating a Balanced Meal Plan

A balanced meal plan can support mental health and help manage PTSD symptoms. Here are some steps to create a nutritious and balanced meal plan:

1. Incorporate a Variety of Nutrient-Rich Foods:
- Fruits and Vegetables: Aim to fill half your plate with a variety of colorful fruits and vegetables. These foods are rich in vitamins, minerals, and antioxidants.

- Whole Grains: Choose whole grains such as brown rice, quinoa, whole wheat bread, and oats. Whole grains provide complex carbohydrates and fibre.
- Lean Proteins: Include lean protein sources such as chicken, turkey, fish, eggs, beans, and legumes. Protein is essential for brain function and overall health.
- Healthy Fats: Incorporate healthy fats from sources like avocados, nuts, seeds, and olive oil. Healthy fats support brain health and reduce inflammation.

2. Plan Balanced Meals and Snacks:
- Breakfast: Start the day with a balanced breakfast that includes protein, whole grains, and fruits or vegetables. Examples include a smoothie with spinach, berries, and protein powder or oatmeal topped with nuts and fruit.
- Lunch: Opt for a balanced lunch that includes lean protein, whole grains, and vegetables. Examples include a quinoa salad with grilled chicken and vegetables or a whole grain wrap with hummus, veggies, and turkey.
- Dinner: Include a variety of foods in your dinner, such as lean protein, whole grains, and vegetables. Examples include grilled salmon with brown rice and steamed broccoli or a stir-fry with tofu, vegetables, and quinoa.
- Snacks: Choose healthy snacks that provide sustained energy and nutrients. Examples include Greek yogurt with berries, a handful of nuts, or sliced vegetables with hummus.

3. Stay Hydrated:
- Drink plenty of water throughout the day to stay hydrated. Aim for at least 8 glasses of water daily.
- Include water-rich foods such as fruits and vegetables in your diet to help maintain hydration.

4. Plan and Prepare Meals Ahead of Time:
- Plan your meals for the week and create a shopping list to ensure you have all the ingredients you need.
- Prepare meals and snacks in advance to make healthy eating

more convenient and reduce the temptation to choose less nutritious options.

5. Practice Mindful Eating:
- Pay attention to your hunger and fullness cues and eat slowly to savor your food.
- Avoid distractions such as TV or phones while eating to fully enjoy your meals and be more aware of your eating habits.

After being diagnosed with PTSD, Mike realized that his diet was impacting his mood and energy levels. He worked with a nutritionist to create a balanced meal plan that included a variety of nutrient-rich foods. By planning his meals and snacks ahead of time, Mike found it easier to make healthy choices. He also practiced mindful eating, which helped him enjoy his food and be more aware of his eating habits. The balanced meal plan supported Mike's mental health and provided him with the energy he needed to manage his symptoms.

Creating a balanced meal plan involves incorporating a variety of nutrient-rich foods, planning balanced meals and snacks, staying hydrated, and practicing mindful eating. By following these steps, individuals can support their mental and physical health and manage PTSD symptoms more effectively.

Nourishing the Mind and Body

After surviving a traumatic event, Rachel found herself struggling with severe anxiety and depression. She realized that her diet was affecting her mood and energy levels, and decided to focus on nutrition as part of her recovery journey.

Rachel began by consulting a nutritionist who helped her develop a balanced meal plan. She incorporated a variety of nutrient-rich foods into her diet, including plenty of fruits and vegetables, lean proteins, whole grains, and healthy fats. Rachel also added supplements such as omega-3 fish oil and a B-complex vitamin to support her mental health.

As she made these dietary changes, Rachel noticed significant improvements in her mood and overall well-being. The balanced diet provided her with sustained energy throughout the day, helping her feel more focused and alert. The omega-3 supplements helped reduce her anxiety, while the B vitamins supported her cognitive function and mood regulation.

Rachel also practiced mindful eating, paying attention to her hunger and fullness cues and savoring each bite of her food. This practice helped her develop a healthier relationship with food and enjoy her meals more fully.

In addition to her balanced diet, Rachel made sure to stay hydrated by drinking plenty of water and incorporating water-rich foods into her meals. She found that staying hydrated improved her energy levels and helped her feel more refreshed.

By nourishing her mind and body with a balanced diet and supplements, Rachel was able to manage her PTSD symptoms more effectively. The dietary changes supported her mental health and provided her with the resilience she needed to navigate her recovery journey.

Rachel's story highlights the importance of nutrition in managing PTSD and supporting overall well-being. By focusing on a balanced diet and mindful eating, individuals can enhance their mental and physical health and find a path to healing.

Nourishing the mind and body with a balanced diet and supplements can provide valuable support for individuals with PTSD. By making informed food choices and practicing mindful eating, individuals can improve their mental health and overall well-being.

CHAPTER 10: CREATIVE THERAPIES

Creative therapies offer unique and powerful ways to express and process emotions, especially for individuals with PTSD. These therapies can provide a safe outlet for feelings that might be difficult to articulate through traditional talk therapy.

Art Therapy:

1. What is Art Therapy?
   - Art therapy involves using visual art-making processes to explore emotions, reduce anxiety, and increase self-awareness. It is facilitated by a trained art therapist who guides individuals in expressing themselves through various art mediums.

2. Benefits of Art Therapy:
   - Emotional Expression: Art therapy provides a non-verbal way to express complex emotions and experiences that might be difficult to put into words.
   - Stress Reduction: Engaging in creative activities can reduce stress and promote relaxation. The act of creating art can be calming and therapeutic.
   - Self-Exploration: Art therapy encourages self-reflection and insight. Creating art can help individuals understand their emotions and experiences more deeply.
   - Improved Self-Esteem: Completing art projects and seeing tangible results can boost self-esteem and provide a sense of accomplishment.

3. Techniques in Art Therapy:

- Drawing and Painting: Using different mediums such as pencils, markers, watercolours, and acrylics to create expressive artworks.

- Collage Making: Combining various materials like magazine cutouts, photographs, and fabric to create a visual narrative.

- Sculpting: Working with clay, playdough, or other sculpting materials to create three-dimensional forms.

- Mandala Creation: Drawing or colouring mandalas (circular designs) to promote focus and mindfulness.

After experiencing a traumatic event, Lisa struggled with severe anxiety and depression. She started attending art therapy sessions where she could express her emotions through painting. The creative process helped Lisa release her pent-up feelings and gain a deeper understanding of her trauma. Art therapy became a safe space for her to explore her emotions and begin her healing journey.

Art therapy offers a valuable way for individuals with PTSD to express themselves and process their emotions. By engaging in creative activities, individuals can find new ways to cope with their trauma and promote their overall well-being.

Music Therapy

Music therapy is another form of creative therapy that can have profound effects on individuals with PTSD. It involves using music to address emotional, cognitive, and social needs.
What is Music Therapy?
- Music therapy is facilitated by a trained music therapist who uses music interventions to help individuals achieve therapeutic goals. These interventions can include listening to music, creating music, singing, and moving to music.

Benefits of Music Therapy:
- Emotional Expression: Music therapy provides a way to express emotions non-verbally. Music can evoke powerful emotions and help individuals process their feelings.

- Stress Reduction: Listening to or creating music can reduce stress and promote relaxation. Music has a soothing effect that can help alleviate anxiety.
- Enhanced Mood: Music can elevate mood and provide a sense of joy and comfort. It can be a positive distraction from negative thoughts and feelings.
- Social Connection: Group music therapy sessions can promote social interaction and build a sense of community. Making music with others can foster a sense of belonging.

Techniques in Music Therapy:
- Listening to Music: Using pre-recorded music to evoke emotions, relax, or energize. Therapists may create personalized playlists based on the individual's preferences and therapeutic needs.
- Playing Instruments: Using instruments such as drums, guitars, or keyboards to create music. This can be a powerful way to express emotions and release physical tension.
- Songwriting: Composing original songs or writing lyrics to express personal experiences and emotions. Songwriting can be a cathartic and empowering process.
- Movement to Music: Incorporating movement and dance to music to enhance physical expression and release pent-up energy.

John, a military veteran with PTSD, found solace in music therapy. He initially struggled to open up about his experiences, but through playing the guitar and writing songs, he was able to express his emotions. Music therapy sessions provided John with a sense of relief and helped him connect with others who shared similar struggles. The power of music became a key component of his healing journey.

Music therapy offers a unique and effective way for individuals with PTSD to explore their emotions and find healing through music. By engaging in musical activities, individuals can improve their emotional well-being and build connections with others.

Dance and Movement Therapy

Dance and movement therapy, also known as dance/movement therapy (DMT), uses movement to help individuals express themselves and address emotional and psychological challenges. This form of therapy can be particularly beneficial for individuals with PTSD.

What is Dance and Movement Therapy?
- DMT is facilitated by trained therapists who use movement to promote emotional, cognitive, and physical integration. It involves using dance and movement as a form of expression and communication.

Benefits of Dance and Movement Therapy:
- Emotional Release: Movement can help release pent-up emotions and provide a physical outlet for feelings that may be difficult to express verbally.
- Stress Reduction: Engaging in dance and movement can reduce stress and promote relaxation. Physical activity stimulates the release of endorphins, which improve mood.
- Body Awareness: DMT enhances body awareness and helps individuals connect with their physical selves. This can be particularly helpful for individuals who have experienced trauma and feel disconnected from their bodies.
- Improved Self-Esteem: Successfully engaging in dance and movement activities can boost self-esteem and provide a sense of accomplishment.
- Social Connection: Group DMT sessions foster social interaction and create a sense of community. Moving together can build trust and connection among participants.

Techniques in Dance and Movement Therapy:
- Improvisational Dance: Encouraging spontaneous movement and dance to express emotions and thoughts. This technique allows for creative expression and exploration.

- Structured Movement: Using specific movement sequences and exercises to promote relaxation, coordination, and body awareness.
- Mirroring: Therapists mirror the movements of participants to build rapport and encourage self-awareness. This technique can enhance empathy and understanding.
- Movement Rituals: Creating rituals and routines that incorporate movement to promote grounding and stability. These rituals can provide a sense of structure and safety.

After surviving a traumatic event, Sarah struggled with anxiety and felt disconnected from her body. She started attending dance and movement therapy sessions where she could express herself through movement. The sessions helped Sarah release her emotions and reconnect with her physical self. Dance and movement therapy provided Sarah with a new way to process her trauma and find healing.

Dance and movement therapy offers a powerful way for individuals with PTSD to express themselves and connect with their bodies. Through movement, individuals can find emotional release, reduce stress, and improve their overall well-being.

Writing as Therapy

Writing can be a powerful therapeutic tool for individuals with PTSD. It provides a safe and private way to explore and express emotions, process traumatic experiences, and gain insights into one's thoughts and feelings.

What is Writing Therapy?
- Writing therapy involves using writing as a therapeutic process. This can include journaling, expressive writing, poetry, and storytelling. It allows individuals to articulate their thoughts and emotions in a structured or unstructured format.

Benefits of Writing Therapy:

- Emotional Expression: Writing provides a way to express complex emotions and thoughts that may be difficult to verbalize. It can help individuals release pent-up feelings and gain emotional clarity.
- Processing Trauma: Writing about traumatic experiences can help individuals process and integrate these events into their life narrative. This can reduce the emotional intensity of the trauma and promote healing.
- Stress Reduction: Writing can be a calming and meditative practice. It helps individuals organize their thoughts and reduce anxiety.
- Self-Reflection: Writing encourages self-reflection and introspection. It helps individuals gain insights into their behavior, thoughts, and feelings.
- Improved Communication: Regular writing can enhance communication skills and improve the ability to articulate emotions and experiences.

Techniques in Writing Therapy:
- Journaling: Keeping a regular journal to document thoughts, feelings, and experiences. Journaling can be a daily practice or used as needed.
- Expressive Writing: Writing about traumatic experiences, focusing on emotions and personal insights. This technique encourages individuals to explore their deepest thoughts and feelings.
- Poetry: Writing poems to express emotions and experiences creatively. Poetry can provide a unique and powerful way to articulate feelings.
- Storytelling: Creating narratives or stories based on personal experiences. Storytelling can help individuals make sense of their trauma and see their experiences from different perspectives.

After experiencing a traumatic event, Michael struggled to talk about his feelings. He started keeping a journal where he could write about his thoughts and emotions privately. The act of writing helped Michael process his trauma and gain a better understanding of his feelings. Over time, writing became a therapeutic practice that supported his emotional healing.

Writing as therapy offers a versatile and accessible way for individuals with PTSD to explore their emotions and process their experiences. Through writing, individuals can find clarity, reduce stress, and promote emotional well-being.

Expressing Through Creativity

After enduring a traumatic experience, Emily found herself overwhelmed by anxiety and depression. Traditional talk therapy provided some relief, but Emily felt she needed additional ways to express her emotions. She decided to explore various creative therapies to support her healing journey.

Emily began with art therapy, where she could use painting and drawing to express her feelings. The process of creating art allowed her to release emotions that she struggled to articulate. Through art therapy sessions, Emily discovered a new way to communicate and process her trauma.

Music therapy also became a significant part of Emily's recovery. She found comfort in listening to calming music and playing the piano. The music provided a soothing escape from

her anxiety and helped her connect with her emotions on a deeper level. Writing and composing her own songs became a powerful outlet for her feelings.

In addition to art and music therapy, Emily participated in dance and movement therapy. The physical expression through dance helped her reconnect with her body and release tension. Moving to music allowed Emily to explore her emotions in a dynamic and embodied way.

Writing therapy was another creative outlet that Emily

embraced. She kept a journal where she could freely express her thoughts and feelings. Writing helped her make sense of her experiences and provided a private space for self-reflection. Poetry and storytelling became tools for Emily to articulate her journey and gain insights into her healing process.

Through these creative therapies, Emily found multiple ways to express and process her emotions. Each form of therapy offered unique benefits and supported different aspects of her recovery. The combination of art, music, dance, and writing provided Emily with a holistic approach to healing.

Emily's story highlights the transformative power of creative therapies in managing PTSD. By engaging in various forms of creative expression, individuals can find new ways to explore their emotions, reduce stress, and promote overall well-being. Creativity can be a powerful tool for healing, offering diverse and accessible methods for emotional expression and recovery.

Expressing through creativity offers individuals with PTSD a valuable and effective way to process their emotions and experiences. By exploring different creative therapies, individuals can enhance their emotional resilience and find a path to healing.

CHAPTER 11: FINDING PURPOSE AND MEANING

Finding purpose and meaning is a crucial component of recovery for individuals with PTSD. A sense of purpose can provide direction, motivation, and a sense of fulfillment, which are essential for overall well-being and long-term recovery.

The Importance of Purpose in Recovery:

1. Motivation and Direction: Having a sense of purpose gives individuals something to strive for and work towards. It provides a reason to get out of bed each day and a framework for making decisions and setting priorities.

2. Resilience and Coping: A strong sense of purpose can enhance resilience, helping individuals cope with the challenges and setbacks that come with recovery. It provides a sense of inner strength and determination to overcome obstacles.

3. Positive Outlook: Finding purpose can shift focus from past traumas to future possibilities. It fosters a positive outlook and encourages individuals to envision and work towards a fulfilling life.

4. Connection and Community: Purpose often involves connecting with others and contributing to something larger than oneself. This can lead to a greater sense of community, belonging, and support.

5. Personal Growth: Pursuing meaningful goals and activities can lead to personal growth and self-discovery. It encourages individuals to explore their interests, values, and passions, fostering a deeper understanding of themselves.

After experiencing a traumatic event, John felt lost and struggled to find direction in his life. Through therapy, he began to explore what was truly important to him and what gave his life meaning. John discovered a passion for helping others and decided to volunteer at a local shelter. This gave him a sense of purpose and fulfillment, which played a significant role in his recovery. Volunteering not only helped John connect with his community but also provided him with a positive focus and motivation.

Finding purpose and meaning is a powerful aspect of recovery. It provides individuals with direction, motivation, and a sense of fulfillment, helping them navigate their healing journey and build a meaningful life.

Setting Goals and Creating a Vision

Setting goals and creating a vision for the future are essential steps in finding purpose and meaning. These steps help individuals focus their efforts, track their progress, and stay motivated throughout their recovery journey.

Steps to Setting Goals and Creating a Vision:
1. Reflect on Values and Passions:
   - Take time to reflect on what is truly important to you. Consider your values, passions, and interests. These reflections can guide you in identifying meaningful goals and creating a vision for your future.

2. Identify Long-Term Goals:
   - Think about where you want to be in the future. What are your aspirations and dreams? Identifying long-term goals provides a sense of direction and purpose.

3. Break Down Goals into Manageable Steps:
   - Once you have identified your long-term goals, break them down into smaller, manageable steps. This makes the goals more achievable and allows you to track your progress.

4. Set SMART Goals:
   - SMART goals are Specific, Measurable, Achievable, Relevant, and Time-bound. Setting SMART goals helps ensure that your objectives are clear and attainable.

5. Create a Vision Board:
   - A vision board is a visual representation of your goals and aspirations. Use images, words, and symbols that resonate with you and represent what you want to achieve. A vision board can serve as a daily reminder of your goals and keep you motivated.

6. Develop an Action Plan:
   - Create an action plan outlining the steps you need to take to achieve your goals. Include specific tasks, deadlines, and resources needed. An action plan provides a roadmap for reaching your objectives.

7. Monitor Progress and Adjust as Needed:
   - Regularly review your goals and action plan. Monitor your progress and adjust as needed. Celebrate your achievements and stay flexible in adapting your goals as circumstances change.

Emily struggled with PTSD after a traumatic event and felt directionless in her recovery. Her therapist suggested setting goals and creating a vision for her future. Emily reflected on her passions and realized she wanted to pursue a career in nursing. She set SMART goals, such as enrolling in a nursing program and completing her studies within three years. Emily created a vision board with images of nurses, medical equipment, and motivational quotes. This visual representation kept her focused and motivated. By breaking down her goals into manageable steps and developing an action plan, Emily was able to stay on track and make significant progress in her recovery.

Setting goals and creating a vision provide individuals with a sense of direction and purpose. By breaking down goals into manageable steps and developing an action plan, individuals can stay focused and motivated in their recovery journey.

Volunteering and Giving Back

Volunteering and giving back to the community can be powerful ways to find purpose and meaning. These activities provide opportunities to make a positive impact, connect with others, and gain a sense of fulfillment.

Benefits of Volunteering and Giving Back:

1. Sense of Purpose: Volunteering provides a meaningful way to contribute to the community and make a difference in the lives of others. It offers a sense of purpose and fulfillment.

2. Social Connection: Volunteering allows individuals to connect with others who share similar interests and values. It fosters a sense of community and belonging.

3. Personal Growth: Volunteering can lead to personal growth and self-discovery. It provides opportunities to develop new skills, gain new experiences, and build confidence.

4. Improved Mental Health: Giving back to others can enhance mental health and well-being. It promotes positive emotions, reduces stress, and increases feelings of happiness and satisfaction.

5. Building Resilience: Volunteering can help individuals build resilience by providing a sense of accomplishment and reinforcing their ability to make a positive impact.

Ways to Get Involved in Volunteering:

1. Identify Your Interests: Consider what causes or issues you are passionate about. This could include working with children,

supporting environmental initiatives, helping the elderly, or advocating for social justice.

2. Research Opportunities: Look for volunteer opportunities in your community that align with your interests. Local non-profits, community centers, schools, and hospitals often have volunteer programs.

3. Reach Out to Organizations: Contact organizations that interest you and inquire about volunteer opportunities. Many organizations have volunteer coordinators who can provide information and guide you through the application process.

4. Start Small: Begin with small, manageable commitments. This allows you to ease into volunteering and see how it fits into your schedule and interests.

5. Consider Virtual Volunteering: If in-person volunteering is not feasible, explore virtual volunteering opportunities. Many organizations offer ways to contribute remotely through online platforms.

6. Join a Group: Consider joining a volunteer group or club. This can provide additional support and social connections, making the experience more enjoyable and rewarding.

After overcoming PTSD, Mike wanted to give back to the community and help others. He decided to volunteer at a local shelter that provided support to homeless individuals. Through volunteering, Mike found a renewed sense of purpose and fulfillment. He connected with like-minded individuals and made a positive impact on the lives of those he helped. Volunteering not only enhanced Mike's mental health but also reinforced his sense of resilience and ability to contribute to the community.

Volunteering and giving back provide valuable opportunities to find purpose and meaning. By contributing to the community and helping others, individuals can enhance their well-being and build connections.

Exploring Spirituality and Faith

Exploring spirituality and faith can be an important aspect of finding purpose and meaning, especially for individuals with PTSD. Spiritual practices and beliefs can provide comfort, guidance, and a sense of connection to something greater than oneself.

Benefits of Spirituality and Faith:

1. Comfort and Hope: Spirituality and faith can offer comfort and hope during difficult times. Beliefs and practices can provide a sense of peace and reassurance.

2. Sense of Purpose: Spirituality and faith often involve a sense of purpose and meaning beyond the self. This can provide direction and motivation in life.

3. Community and Support: Many spiritual and religious traditions involve community gatherings and support networks. These communities can provide emotional and social support.

4. Personal Growth: Exploring spirituality and faith can lead to personal growth and self-discovery. It encourages reflection, introspection, and a deeper understanding of oneself.

5. Resilience and Coping: Spiritual beliefs and practices can enhance resilience and coping skills. They provide a framework for understanding and navigating life's challenges.

Ways to Explore Spirituality and Faith:

1. Reflect on Beliefs: Take time to reflect on your beliefs and values. Consider what spirituality and faith mean to you and how they can support your recovery.

2. Engage in Practices: Explore spiritual practices that resonate with you. This could include prayer, meditation, reading sacred

texts, or attending religious services.

3. Connect with Communities: Join spiritual or religious communities that align with your beliefs. Engaging with others who share similar values can provide support and connection.

4. Seek Guidance: Consider seeking guidance from spiritual leaders or mentors. They can offer insights, support, and resources to help you explore your spirituality and faith.

5. Practice Mindfulness: Incorporate mindfulness practices into your spiritual journey. Mindfulness can enhance spiritual awareness and deepen your connection to your beliefs.

6. Explore Nature: Many individuals find spirituality in nature. Spending time outdoors and appreciating the natural world can provide a sense of awe and connection to something greater.

After experiencing a traumatic event, Sarah struggled to find meaning and purpose in her life. She decided to explore her spirituality and joined a local meditation group. Through meditation and reflection, Sarah found a sense of peace and connection to something greater than herself. The spiritual practices provided comfort and guidance, helping her navigate her recovery. Connecting with the meditation community also offered support and a sense of belonging. Spirituality became an integral part of Sarah's healing journey, providing her with purpose and meaning.

Exploring spirituality and faith can provide valuable support for individuals with PTSD. By engaging in spiritual practices and connecting with communities, individuals can find comfort, purpose, and resilience.

Rediscovering Life's Meaning

After surviving a traumatic event, David felt disconnected and struggled to find purpose in his life. He was overwhelmed by feelings of emptiness and uncertainty. Determined to reclaim his sense of meaning, David embarked on a journey of self-discovery and healing.

David began by setting small, achievable goals that aligned with his interests and passions. He reflected on what was truly important to him and identified long-term goals that provided a sense of direction. David created a vision board filled with images and words that represented his aspirations, which served as a daily reminder of his goals.

Volunteering became a significant part of David's journey. He joined a local organization that supported veterans and found fulfillment in helping others who had experienced similar challenges. The sense of purpose and connection he gained from volunteering was profound and provided him with a renewed sense of meaning.

David also explored his spirituality, seeking comfort and guidance through meditation and reflection. He joined a meditation group where he connected with others who shared similar values. The spiritual practices offered David a sense of peace and resilience, helping him navigate his recovery.

Through these experiences, David rediscovered his life's meaning. He found that setting goals, giving back to the community, and exploring his spirituality provided him with a sense of purpose and fulfillment. David's journey was not without challenges, but the support of his community and his commitment to personal growth helped him overcome obstacles.

David's story highlights the importance of finding purpose and meaning in recovery. By setting goals, volunteering, and exploring spirituality, individuals can reclaim their sense of direction and build a fulfilling life. David's experience demonstrates that it is possible to rediscover life's meaning and find hope and healing after trauma.

Rediscovering life's meaning involves exploring what is truly important, setting meaningful goals, giving back to the community, and connecting with spirituality. By engaging in these activities, individuals with PTSD can find purpose, resilience, and fulfillment.

CHAPTER 12: NAVIGATING RELATIONSHIPS

PTSD can have a profound impact on relationships, affecting communication, trust, and emotional intimacy. Understanding these effects and learning how to navigate them is crucial for building and maintaining healthy relationships.

The Impact of PTSD on Relationships:

1. Emotional Distance: Individuals with PTSD may experience emotional numbness or detachment, making it challenging to connect with loved ones. This can lead to feelings of isolation and loneliness for both parties.

2. Communication Barriers: PTSD can affect communication, leading to misunderstandings and conflicts. Individuals may have difficulty expressing their feelings or may avoid conversations that trigger distress.

3. Trust Issues: Trauma can erode trust, making it difficult for individuals with PTSD to feel safe and secure in their relationships. This can lead to suspicion, jealousy, and a need for constant reassurance.

4. Hypervigilance and Anxiety: PTSD often involves heightened anxiety and hypervigilance, which can strain relationships. Loved ones may feel they are walking on eggshells, unsure of how to provide support without triggering anxiety.

5. Irritability and Anger: PTSD can lead to increased irritability and anger outbursts, which can be challenging for partners and family members to navigate. These outbursts may be misunderstood or seen as unwarranted aggression.

6. Avoidance Behaviors: Individuals with PTSD may avoid places, activities, or people that remind them of their trauma. This can limit social interactions and strain relationships.

After returning from deployment, James struggled with PTSD and found it difficult to connect with his wife, Emily. He often felt emotionally numb and avoided conversations about his experiences. Emily felt isolated and unsure of how to support him. They began attending couples therapy, where they learned about the impact of PTSD on their relationship and developed strategies to improve communication and rebuild trust.

Understanding the impact of PTSD on relationships is the first step toward navigating these challenges. By acknowledging these effects and seeking support, individuals and their loved ones can work together to build stronger, healthier relationships.

Communicating Effectively with Loved Ones

Effective communication is essential for maintaining healthy relationships, especially when navigating the challenges of PTSD. Open and honest communication can help build understanding, trust, and emotional intimacy.

Strategies for Effective Communication:

1. Active Listening: Practice active listening by giving your full attention to your partner or loved one. Avoid interrupting and show empathy by acknowledging their feelings and experiences.

2. Expressing Feelings: Use "I" statements to express your feelings without placing blame. For example, "I feel anxious when we talk about this topic" instead of "You make me

anxious."

3. Setting Aside Time for Conversations: Schedule regular times to talk without distractions. This dedicated time can help ensure that important conversations are not overlooked.

4. Being Honest and Open: Share your thoughts and feelings honestly, even if they are difficult to discuss. Honesty builds trust and fosters deeper connections.

5. Avoiding Assumptions: Avoid making assumptions about what the other person is thinking or feeling. Instead, ask questions to clarify and understand their perspective.

6. Using Nonverbal Communication: Pay attention to nonverbal cues, such as body language and facial expressions. Nonverbal communication can convey empathy and support.

7. Staying Calm: Try to remain calm during difficult conversations. Take deep breaths and pause if needed to collect your thoughts.

8. Seeking Professional Help: If communication challenges persist, consider seeking the help of a therapist or counselor who can provide guidance and support.

Sarah and her husband, Mark, struggled with communication after she was diagnosed with PTSD. Mark often felt helpless and unsure of how to support Sarah, while Sarah felt misunderstood and isolated. They decided to work on their communication skills by practicing active listening and setting aside time for regular conversations. With time and effort, they were able to rebuild their connection and improve their relationship.

Effective communication is key to navigating the challenges of PTSD in relationships. By practicing active listening, expressing feelings honestly, and seeking professional help if needed, individuals can build stronger, more supportive relationships.

Building Healthy Boundaries

Establishing and maintaining healthy boundaries is crucial for individuals with PTSD and their loved ones. Boundaries help protect emotional well-being, promote mutual respect, and ensure that relationships are supportive and balanced.

Importance of Healthy Boundaries:

1. Protecting Emotional Well-Being: Boundaries help individuals manage their emotional energy and avoid feeling overwhelmed. They provide a sense of safety and control.

2. Promoting Mutual Respect: Boundaries ensure that both parties respect each other's needs and limits. This fosters a healthier and more respectful relationship.

3. Preventing Resentment: Clear boundaries help prevent feelings of resentment that can arise when personal limits are crossed or ignored.

4. Encouraging Independence: Boundaries promote independence and self-care, allowing individuals to take responsibility for their own well-being.

Tips for Building Healthy Boundaries:

1. Identify Your Needs: Reflect on your needs and what boundaries are necessary to protect your emotional well-being. Consider areas where you feel uncomfortable or overwhelmed.

2. Communicate Clearly: Clearly communicate your boundaries to your loved ones. Use "I" statements to express your needs and explain why these boundaries are important to you.

3. Be Consistent: Consistently enforce your boundaries. If a boundary is crossed, address it calmly and assertively. Consistency helps reinforce the importance of your limits.

4. Respect Others' Boundaries: Just as you set boundaries for yourself, respect the boundaries of others. This mutual respect is essential for maintaining healthy relationships.

5. Practice Self-Care: Prioritize self-care and ensure that your boundaries allow time for rest, relaxation, and activities that nurture your well-being.

6. Seek Support: If setting and maintaining boundaries is challenging, seek support from a therapist or counselor. They can provide guidance and help you develop effective boundary-setting skills.

After being diagnosed with PTSD, Emily realized that she needed to set boundaries to protect her emotional well-being. She communicated her needs to her family, explaining that she needed time alone after therapy sessions to process her emotions. Emily also set boundaries around social activities, only attending events that felt manageable. By setting and maintaining these boundaries, Emily was able to manage her symptoms more effectively and feel more in control of her recovery.

Building healthy boundaries is essential for individuals with PTSD and their loved ones. By identifying needs, communicating clearly, and practicing self-care, individuals can create supportive and balanced relationships.

Relationship Counseling and Therapy

Relationship counseling and therapy can provide valuable support for couples and families navigating the challenges of PTSD. Professional guidance can help improve communication, rebuild trust, and strengthen emotional connections.

Benefits of Relationship Counseling and Therapy:

1. Improved Communication: Therapists can teach effective communication skills and provide a safe space for open and honest conversations. This can help couples and families understand each other better and resolve conflicts.

2. Rebuilding Trust: Therapy can address issues of trust that

may have been damaged by trauma. Therapists can guide couples in rebuilding trust and creating a secure and supportive relationship.

3. Emotional Support: Therapy provides a space for individuals to express their emotions and receive support. This can be particularly important for individuals with PTSD who may struggle with emotional expression.

4. Conflict Resolution: Therapists can help couples and families develop strategies for resolving conflicts in a healthy and constructive manner. This can reduce tension and improve relationship dynamics.

5. Strengthening Connections: Therapy can help couples and families strengthen their emotional connections and foster a sense of intimacy and closeness.

Types of Relationship Therapy:

1. Couples Therapy: Couples therapy focuses on improving the relationship between partners. It addresses issues such as communication, trust, intimacy, and conflict resolution.

2. Family Therapy: Family therapy involves working with the entire family to improve communication, resolve conflicts, and address the impact of PTSD on family dynamics.

3. Group Therapy: Group therapy involves multiple couples or families working together with a therapist. It provides opportunities for shared experiences, mutual support, and learning from others.

4. Individual Therapy: Individual therapy can also be beneficial for relationship issues. It allows individuals to work on personal challenges that may affect their relationships.

After experiencing trauma, Lisa and her husband, Tom, found it difficult to communicate and maintain their emotional connection. They decided to attend couples therapy to address these challenges. Through therapy, they learned effective communication skills and worked on rebuilding trust. The therapist provided a safe space for them to express their feelings and resolve conflicts. Over time, Lisa and Tom's relationship improved, and they felt more connected and supported.

Relationship counseling and therapy offer valuable tools and support for couples and families navigating the challenges of PTSD. By improving communication, rebuilding trust, and strengthening connections, therapy can help create healthier and more supportive relationships.

Rebuilding Connections

After returning from military service, Mike struggled with severe PTSD that affected his relationship with his wife, Karen. He often felt emotionally distant and had difficulty communicating his feelings. Karen felt isolated and unsure of how to support Mike. They both knew they needed help to rebuild their connection.

Mike and Karen decided to attend couples therapy to address the impact of PTSD on their relationship. The therapist helped them understand how trauma was affecting their communication and emotional intimacy. Through therapy, they learned effective communication techniques, such as active listening and using "I" statements to express their feelings.

The therapist also guided them in setting healthy boundaries and developing strategies for managing Mike's PTSD symptoms. This included creating a safe space for Mike to process his emotions and setting aside regular time for meaningful conversations.

In addition to couples therapy, Mike attended individual therapy to work on his personal challenges. This helped him gaininsights into his trauma and develop coping strategies. Karen joined a support group for spouses of veterans with PTSD, where she found comfort and understanding from others who shared similar experiences.

Over time, Mike and Karen's relationship began to improve. They felt more connected and understood each other's needs better. The combination of couples therapy, individual therapy, and support groups provided them with the tools and support they needed to rebuild their connection.

Mike's journey highlights the importance of seeking professional help and building a support network. By addressing the impact of PTSD on their relationship and working together, Mike and Karen were able to strengthen their bond and create a healthier, more supportive relationship.

Rebuilding connections after trauma requires effort, communication, and support. By seeking therapy and working together, individuals with PTSD and their loved ones can navigate challenges and create meaningful and fulfilling relationships.

CHAPTER 13: COPING WITH RELAPSES

Relapses are a common part of the recovery process for individuals with PTSD. Understanding why they happen and how to cope with them is crucial for long-term recovery and resilience.

Understanding Relapses in PTSD:

1. What is a Relapse?
   - A relapse occurs when symptoms of PTSD that have been managed or reduced return or worsen. This can happen suddenly or gradually and can be triggered by various factors.

2. Common Causes of Relapse:
   - Triggers: Specific situations, environments, or memories that remind individuals of their trauma can trigger a relapse. These triggers can be external (e.g., certain places or sounds) or internal (e.g., thoughts or emotions).
   - Stress: Increased stress, whether from personal, professional, or environmental sources, can exacerbate PTSD symptoms and lead to a relapse.
   - Changes in Routine: Significant changes in daily routine, such as moving to a new place, changing jobs, or experiencing a loss, can disrupt coping mechanisms and trigger a relapse.
   - Physical Health Issues: Illness, injury, or changes in physical health can impact mental health and contribute to a relapse.

3. The Emotional Impact of Relapse:
   - Experiencing a relapse can be discouraging and frustrating.

It may lead to feelings of hopelessness, guilt, or self-blame. Understanding that relapses are a normal part of the recovery process can help mitigate these negative emotions.

4. The Recovery Process:

   - Recovery from PTSD is not a linear process. It involves progress, setbacks, and continuous effort. Relapses are part of this journey and provide opportunities for learning and growth.

After years of managing her PTSD symptoms, Maria experienced a relapse triggered by a stressful job change. She felt overwhelmed and discouraged, fearing she was back to square one. Her therapist helped Maria understand that relapses are a normal part of recovery. Together, they identified the triggers and developed strategies to manage her symptoms. Maria's experience taught her that setbacks are temporary and part of the healing process.

Understanding relapses in PTSD is the first step toward managing them effectively. By recognizing that relapses are a normal part of recovery, individuals can approach setbacks with resilience and a proactive mindset.

Early Warning Signs and Triggers

Recognizing the early warning signs and triggers of a PTSD relapse can help individuals take proactive steps to manage their symptoms and prevent a full-blown relapse.

Common Early Warning Signs:

1. Increased Anxiety: A noticeable increase in anxiety or nervousness can be an early sign of a potential relapse. This may manifest as restlessness, excessive worrying, or difficulty concentrating.

2. Changes in Sleep Patterns: Disruptions in sleep, such as difficulty falling asleep, frequent waking, or nightmares, can indicate that a relapse is imminent.

3. Emotional Numbness: Feeling emotionally numb or detached from others can be a warning sign. This may involve a lack of interest in activities, decreased emotional expression, or withdrawal from social interactions.

4. Irritability and Anger: Increased irritability, frustration, or anger outbursts can signal that PTSD symptoms are resurfacing.

5. Avoidance Behaviors: Avoiding places, activities, or people that are reminders of the trauma can be an early indicator of a relapse. This may also include avoiding thoughts or conversations about the trauma.

6. Negative Thoughts: An increase in negative thoughts or feelings of hopelessness, guilt, or self-blame can be a sign that a relapse is approaching.
Identifying Personal Triggers:

1. External Triggers: These are situations, environments, or stimuli outside the individual that remind them of their trauma. Common external triggers include specific locations, people, sounds, or smells associated with the traumatic event.

2. Internal Triggers: These are thoughts, memories, or emotions that remind the individual of their trauma. Internal triggers can be more subtle and include feelings of fear, anger, or sadness that arise without an obvious external cause.

3. Stressful Life Events: Major life changes or stressful events, such as moving, changing jobs, or experiencing a loss, can act as triggers for a relapse.

4. Anniversaries: Anniversaries of the traumatic event can be particularly challenging and may trigger a relapse. These dates can bring back intense memories and emotions.

Strategies for Identifying Triggers:

1. Keep a Journal: Keeping a journal of daily activities, thoughts,

and emotions can help identify patterns and triggers. Writing down when symptoms increase can provide insights into potential triggers.

2. Reflect on Past Relapses: Reviewing past relapses and identifying what preceded them can help recognize
common triggers. This can inform future strategies for managing symptoms.

3. Seek Feedback: Asking for feedback from trusted friends, family, or a therapist can provide additional perspectives on potential triggers.

After a period of stability, Jake noticed his anxiety levels rising and began experiencing nightmares again. By keeping a journal, he identified that the upcoming anniversary of his trauma was triggering these symptoms. With this awareness, Jake worked with his therapist to develop a plan to manage his symptoms and navigate this difficult time. Recognizing the early warning signs and triggers allowed Jake to take proactive steps to prevent a full relapse.

Identifying early warning signs and triggers is essential for managing PTSD relapses. By being aware of these signs and understanding personal triggers, individuals can take proactive steps to manage their symptoms and maintain their recovery.

Strategies for Managing Relapses

When a PTSD relapse occurs, it is important to have strategies in place to manage the symptoms and mitigate the impact. These strategies can help individuals regain control and continue their recovery journey.

Immediate Coping Strategies:

1. Grounding Techniques: Grounding techniques can help individuals stay present and reduce the intensity of distressing symptoms. Examples include focusing on the five senses, deep

breathing exercises, or repeating a calming phrase.

2. Self-Soothing Activities: Engage in activities that provide comfort and relaxation, such as taking a warm bath, listening to soothing music, or practicing mindfulness meditation.

3. Reach Out for Support: Contact a trusted friend, family member, or therapist for support. Talking about your feelings and experiences can provide emotional relief and a sense of connection.

4. Create a Safe Space: Identify a safe and quiet place where you can retreat to calm down and regroup. This space should be free from triggers and distractions.

Long-Term Management Strategies:

1. Develop a Relapse Prevention Plan: Work with a therapist to create a relapse prevention plan that includes identifying triggers, early warning signs, and coping strategies. This plan can provide a roadmap for managing relapses.

2. Maintain a Routine: Keeping a regular daily routine can provide structure and stability. Include activities that promote physical and mental well-being, such as exercise, healthy eating, and sufficient sleep.

3. Engage in Therapy: Regular therapy sessions can provide ongoing support and help individuals develop effective coping strategies. Therapy can also address underlying issues that contribute to relapses.

4. Practice Self-Compassion: Be kind and patient with yourself during a relapse. Understand that relapses are a normal part of the recovery process and do not define your progress.

5. Stay Connected: Maintain social connections and engage in activities that provide a sense of purpose and fulfillment. Social support is crucial for mental health and can help buffer against the effects of a relapse.

6. Monitor Substance Use: Avoid using alcohol or drugs to cope with symptoms. Substance use can exacerbate PTSD symptoms and increase the risk of relapse.

After experiencing a relapse, Emily felt overwhelmed and unsure of how to cope with her symptoms. She reached out to her therapist, who helped her develop a relapse prevention plan. Emily learned grounding techniques and self-soothing activities that she could use during distressing moments. She also maintained a routine that included regular exercise and mindfulness meditation. By following her relapse prevention plan and practicing self-compassion, Emily was able to manage her symptoms and continue her recovery journey.

Managing relapses involves both immediate coping strategies and long-term management techniques. By developing a relapse prevention plan and engaging in supportive activities, individuals can navigate relapses and maintain their progress.

The Importance of a Relapse Prevention Plan

A relapse prevention plan is a proactive approach to managing PTSD and reducing the likelihood of relapses. This plan provides a structured framework for recognizing triggers, responding to early warning signs, and implementing effective coping strategies.

Components of a Relapse Prevention Plan:

1. Identifying Triggers:
   - List common external and internal triggers that may lead to a relapse. This can include specific places, people, thoughts, or emotions that remind you of your trauma.

2. Recognizing Early Warning Signs:
   - Identify the early warning signs that indicate a potential relapse. This can include changes in mood, behavior, sleep patterns, or physical symptoms.

3. Developing Coping Strategies:
   - Outline specific coping strategies that can be used when early warning signs or triggers are identified. These strategies can include grounding techniques, self-soothing activities, and reaching out for support.

4. Creating a Support Network:
   - Identify trusted friends, family members, or therapists who can provide support during a relapse. Include their contact information in the plan and discuss how they can assist you.

5. Maintaining a Healthy Routine:
   - Establish a daily routine that includes activities that promote physical and mental well-being. This can include regular exercise, healthy eating, sufficient sleep, and mindfulness practices.

6. Setting Goals:
   - Set short-term and long-term goals that provide a sense of purpose and direction. Goals can help maintain motivation and focus during difficult times.

7. Monitoring Substance Use:

-Include strategies for avoiding the use of alcohol or drugs as a coping mechanism. Substance use can worsen PTSD symptoms and increase the risk of relapse.

8. Reviewing and Updating the Plan:
   - Regularly review and update the relapse prevention plan to ensure it remains relevant and effective. Adjust the plan as needed based on new experiences and insights.

Implementing the Relapse Prevention Plan:

1. Keep the Plan Accessible:
   - Ensure that the relapse prevention plan is easily accessible. Consider keeping a copy in a journal, on your phone, or in a place where you can quickly refer to it.

2. Share the Plan with Others:
   - Share the plan with trusted friends, family members, or therapists who can support you during a relapse. Ensure they understand their role in providing assistance.

3. Practice Coping Strategies:
   - Regularly practice the coping strategies outlined in the plan. Familiarity with these techniques can make them more effective when needed.

4. Stay Proactive:
   - Be proactive in monitoring your mental health and recognizing early warning signs. Act as soon as you notice any changes in your symptoms.

After experiencing several relapses, Jake worked with his therapist to develop a relapse prevention plan. The plan included identifying his triggers, recognizing early warning signs, and outlining specific coping strategies. Jake shared the plan with his wife, who provided additional support. By following the plan and staying proactive, Jake was able to manage his symptoms more effectively and reduce the frequency and severity of relapses.

A relapse prevention plan is an essential tool for managing PTSD and maintaining recovery. By identifying triggers, recognizing early warning signs, and implementing effective coping strategies, individuals can navigate relapses and continue their healing journey.

Overcoming Setbacks

After experiencing a traumatic event, Sarah struggled with PTSD and had been making steady progress in her recovery. However, she encountered a significant setback when a stressful work situation triggered a relapse. Sarah felt overwhelmed by anxiety and flashbacks, fearing that all her progress had been undone.

Determined to overcome this setback, Sarah reached out to her therapist for support. Together, they reviewed her relapse prevention plan and identified the triggers and early warning signs that led to the relapse. Sarah realized that the increased stress at work had been a significant factor, and she needed to develop new strategies to manage it.

Sarah's therapist helped her incorporate additional coping techniques into her plan, such as mindfulness meditation and deep breathing exercises. They also discussed the importance of setting healthy boundaries at work to reduce stress. Sarah decided to speak with her supervisor about adjusting her workload and taking regular breaks to manage her anxiety.

In addition to the new coping strategies, Sarah focused on self-care and maintaining a healthy routine. She made time for activities that brought her joy and relaxation, such as gardening and spending time with her pets. Sarah also reconnected with her support network, including friends and family who provided encouragement and understanding.

Despite the initial setback, Sarah's proactive approach and the support of her therapist and loved ones helped her navigate the relapse. She learned that setbacks are a normal part of the recovery process and do not erase the progress she had made. Instead, they provided opportunities for growth and resilience.

Sarah's story highlights the importance of perseverance and self-compassion in overcoming setbacks. By acknowledging the relapse, seeking support, and implementing new strategies, Sarah was able to regain control and continue her recovery journey. Her experience demonstrated that setbacks are temporary and can be overcome with determination and the right support.

Overcoming setbacks involves acknowledging the relapse, seeking support, and implementing effective coping strategies.

By staying proactive and practicing self-compassion, individuals with PTSD can navigate relapses and continue their path to healing.

CHAPTER 14: WORKPLACE STRATEGIES

Managing PTSD in the workplace can be challenging, but with the right strategies, individuals can maintain their productivity and well-being. Understanding how to navigate work-related stressors and seeking support can help create a more balanced and supportive work environment.

Managing PTSD at Work:

1. Recognize Your Triggers: Identify work-related situations or tasks that may trigger your PTSD symptoms. Common triggers can include high-stress projects, specific work environments, or interactions with certain colleagues.

2. Develop Coping Strategies: Implement coping strategies that can help manage symptoms while at work. This can include grounding techniques, deep breathing exercises, and taking short breaks to regroup.

3. Create a Comfortable Workspace: Personalize your workspace to create a calming and comfortable environment. This can include adding plants, personal items, or using noise-cancelling headphones to reduce distractions.

4. Prioritize Self-Care: Ensure that you prioritize self-care activities outside of work hours. This includes getting enough

sleep, maintaining a healthy diet, and engaging in regular physical activity.

5. Manage Workload: Be mindful of your workload and avoid taking on too many tasks at once. Break projects into smaller, manageable steps and set realistic deadlines to reduce stress.

6. Seek Support: Reach out to trusted colleagues or supervisors who can provide support and understanding. Having a support system at work can help you feel more secure and less isolated.

After being diagnosed with PTSD, Emily found it challenging to manage her symptoms at work. She often felt overwhelmed by stress and struggled to concentrate. Emily started implementing coping strategies, such as taking short breaks to practice deep breathing exercises and personalizing her workspace with calming items. She also reached out to her supervisor, who provided additional support and helped adjust her workload. These strategies allowed Emily to manage her symptoms more effectively and maintain her productivity at work.

Managing PTSD at work involves recognizing triggers, implementing coping strategies, and seeking support. By creating a comfortable workspace and prioritizing self-care, individuals can maintain their well-being and thrive in their professional roles.

Disclosure and Seeking Accommodations

Deciding whether to disclose a PTSD diagnosis at work can be difficult. However, disclosure can lead to receiving necessary accommodations and support to manage symptoms more effectively.

Deciding to Disclose:

1. Weigh the Pros and Cons: Consider the potential benefits and risks of disclosing your PTSD diagnosis. Benefits may

include receiving accommodations and support, while risks may include concerns about privacy and potential stigma.

2. Choose the Right Time: Choose an appropriate time to disclose your diagnosis, such as during a private meeting with your supervisor or HR representative. Avoid discussing it during high-stress periods or in public settings.

3. Prepare Your Explanation: Be prepared to explain your diagnosis and how it affects your work. Focus on the specific accommodations you need to manage your symptoms and maintain productivity.

4. Know Your Rights: Familiarize yourself with your rights under workplace laws, such as the Americans with Disabilities Act (ADA). Understanding your legal protections can provide confidence when discussing accommodations.

Seeking Accommodations:

1. Identify Needed Accommodations: Determine the specific accommodations that can help you manage your PTSD symptoms at work. This can include flexible work hours, modified tasks, or access to a quiet space.

2. Request Accommodations Formally: Submit a formal request for accommodations through your company's HR department or your supervisor. Provide documentation from a healthcare provider if required.

3. Work Collaboratively: Collaborate with your supervisor or HR representative to develop a plan that meets your needs while maintaining workplace productivity. Be open to discussing different options and finding mutually beneficial solutions.

4. Monitor and Adjust: Regularly assess the effectiveness of the accommodations and adjust as needed. Communicate any changes in your needs to your supervisor or HR representative.

After struggling with PTSD symptoms at work, John decided

to disclose his diagnosis to his HR department. He explained how his symptoms affected his productivity and requested accommodations, such as flexible work hours and access to a quiet room for breaks. The HR department was supportive and worked with John to implement these accommodations. As a result, John was able to manage his symptoms more effectively and felt more supported in his workplace.

Disclosing a PTSD diagnosis and seeking accommodations can provide valuable support and help manage symptoms at work. By understanding your rights and working collaboratively with your employer, you can create a more supportive and accommodating work environment.

Balancing Work and Mental Health

Maintaining a balance between work and mental health is essential for overall well-being. Implementing strategies to manage stress and prioritize self-care can help individuals with PTSD thrive in the workplace.

Strategies for Balancing Work and Mental Health:

1. Set Boundaries: Establish clear boundaries between work and personal life. Avoid bringing work home and set limits on work-related communications outside of office hours.

2. Take Breaks: Schedule regular breaks throughout the workday to rest and recharge. Short breaks can improve focus and reduce stress.

3. Practice Time Management: Prioritize tasks and manage your time effectively to avoid feeling overwhelmed. Use tools like to-do lists and calendars to stay organized.

4. Engage in Stress-Relief Activities: Incorporate activities that reduce stress into your daily routine. This can include exercise, meditation, hobbies, or spending time with loved ones.

5. Communicate Needs: Communicate your needs to your

employer and colleagues. Let them know if you need additional support or adjustments to manage your workload.

6. Use Employee Assistance Programs (EAP): Take advantage of employee assistance programs that offer mental health resources, counseling, and support services.

Building a Supportive Work Environment:

1. Foster Open Communication: Encourage open communication with colleagues and supervisors. A supportive work environment promotes understanding and reduces stigma.

2. Promote Work-Life Balance: Advocate for policies that promote work-life balance, such as flexible work hours and remote work options.

3. Provide Mental Health Resources: Encourage your employer to provide mental health resources and training. This can include workshops on stress management and access to counseling services.

4. Supportive Leadership: Leaders and managers should model healthy work-life balance and support employees' mental health needs.

After experiencing burnout due to her demanding job, Sarah realized she needed to prioritize her mental health. She set clear boundaries between work and personal life, ensuring she did not check work emails outside of office hours. Sarah also incorporated stress-relief activities, such as yoga and painting, into her routine. She communicated her needs to her supervisor, who supported her by adjusting her workload. By balancing work and mental health, Sarah was able to reduce her stress and improve her overall well-being.

Balancing work and mental health involves setting boundaries, managing time effectively, and prioritizing self-care. By fostering a supportive work environment and communicating needs, individuals with PTSD can thrive in their professional roles while maintaining their mental well-being.

Career Changes and Finding Supportive Environments

For some individuals with PTSD, changing careers or finding a more supportive work environment may be necessary to maintain their mental health and well-being. Exploring different career options and seeking supportive workplaces can provide a fresh start and better align with personal needs.

Considering a Career Change:

1. Assess Your Current Situation: Reflect on your current job and how it impacts your mental health. Identify specific aspects of the job that contribute to stress or exacerbate PTSD symptoms.

2. Explore Interests and Passions: Consider your interests, passions, and skills. Exploring new career paths that align with these areas can lead to greater job satisfaction and well-being.

3. Research Career Options: Research potential career options that may be a better fit for your needs. Consider factors such as work environment, job responsibilities, and company culture.

4. Seek Professional Guidance: Consult with a career counselor or vocational therapist who can provide guidance and support in exploring new career paths and making informed decisions.

5. Develop New Skills: If necessary, pursue additional education or training to develop the skills needed for a new career. This can enhance your qualifications and increase your confidence.

Finding Supportive Work Environments:

1. Research Company Culture: Look for companies that prioritize employee well-being and have a positive work culture. Company reviews, employee testimonials, and company websites can provide insights into the work environment.

2. Inquire About Mental Health Policies: During the interview

process, inquire about the company's mental health policies and support programs. This can include flexible work arrangements, employee assistance programs, and mental health resources.

3. Network with Professionals: Connect with professionals in your desired field to learn more about their experiences and the work environment. Networking can provide valuable insights and potential job opportunities.

4. Evaluate Job Offers: When evaluating job offers, consider not only the salary and benefits but also the work environment and company culture. A supportive work environment is crucial for maintaining mental health.

5. Advocate for Yourself: Once you secure a new job, advocate for your mental health needs. Communicate with your employer about any accommodations or support you may require.

After realizing that her high-stress job was negatively impacting her mental health, Emily decided to explore a career change. She assessed her skills and interests and pursued additional training in graphic design, a field she had always been passionate about. Emily researched companies with positive work cultures and found a supportive design firm that prioritized employee well-being. The new job provided a healthier work environment, allowing Emily to thrive both professionally and personally.

Changing careers and finding supportive work environments can be transformative for individuals with PTSD. By exploring new career paths and prioritizing mental health, individuals can create a fulfilling and supportive professional life.

Thriving in the Workplace

After serving in the military, Tom struggled with PTSD and found it challenging to manage his symptoms while working in a high-stress corporate job. The constant pressure and long hours exacerbated his anxiety and made it difficult to maintain his mental health. Realizing he needed a change; Tom decided to explore different career options and seek a more supportive work environment.

Tom reflected on his interests and skills and discovered a passion for teaching. He pursued additional training and obtained the necessary certifications to become a high school teacher. During his job search, Tom prioritized finding a school with a supportive and positive culture. He connected with other teachers and learned about their experiences, which helped him identify schools that aligned with his values.

Tom eventually secured a teaching position at a school known for its supportive environment and strong emphasis on employee well-being. The school offered flexible work hours, access to mental health resources, and a collaborative community of educators. Tom communicated his needs to the school administration, who provided accommodations to help him manage his PTSD symptoms.

In his new role, Tom found a sense of purpose and fulfillment that had been missing in his previous job. The supportive work environment allowed him to thrive both professionally and personally. He felt more connected to his colleagues and students, which contributed to his overall well-being.

Tom's story demonstrates the importance of finding a career that aligns with one's interests and values and prioritizing mental health in the workplace. By making a career change and seeking a supportive work environment, Tom was able to manage his PTSD symptoms effectively and find satisfaction in his professional life.

Thriving in the workplace involves finding a career that aligns with personal passions and seeking environments that support mental health. By making informed decisions and advocating for their needs, individuals with PTSD can create fulfilling and supportive professional lives.

CHAPTER 15: PARENTING AND PTSD

Parenting with PTSD presents unique challenges, as the symptoms of PTSD can affect one's ability to provide consistent care and support to children. Understanding these challenges and developing strategies to manage them can help parents navigate their roles more effectively.

Parenting with PTSD:

1. Impact on Parenting Abilities:
   - Emotional Regulation: PTSD can affect emotional regulation, making it difficult to remain calm and composed in stressful situations. This can impact the parent-child relationship.
   - Attention and Presence: Symptoms like hypervigilance, flashbacks, and intrusive thoughts can make it challenging to be fully present and attentive to children's needs.
   - Consistency: PTSD symptoms can lead to inconsistent parenting practices, which can confuse children and impact their sense of security.

2. Strategies for Managing Parenting Challenges:
   - Self-Care: Prioritize self-care to manage PTSD symptoms effectively. This includes regular therapy, exercise, healthy eating, and sufficient sleep.
   - Mindfulness Practices: Engage in mindfulness practices to stay grounded and present. Techniques such as deep breathing, meditation, and grounding exercises can help regulate

emotions.

- Set Realistic Expectations: Understand your limitations and set realistic expectations for yourself as a parent. It's okay to seek help and delegate responsibilities when needed.

- Create a Support System: Build a support system of family, friends, and professionals who can aid and understanding. This network can offer practical help and emotional support.

- Establish Routines: Consistent routines can provide stability for both parents and children. Establishing regular mealtimes, bedtimes, and activities can create a sense of predictability and security.

After being diagnosed with PTSD, Laura struggled with emotional regulation and being present for her children. She felt overwhelmed and guilty about not being the parent she wanted to be. Laura started attending therapy and practicing mindfulness exercises to manage her symptoms. She also reached out to her family for support and established consistent routines for her children. These changes helped Laura improve her parenting abilities and strengthen her relationship with her children.

Parenting with PTSD involves recognizing the impact of symptoms on parenting abilities and implementing strategies to manage them. By prioritizing self-care, seeking support, and establishing routines, parents can navigate the challenges of PTSD and provide consistent care for their children.

Supporting Children When a Parent Has PTSD

Children can be deeply affected when a parent has PTSD. Providing them with understanding, reassurance, and support is crucial for their emotional well-being and development.

Understanding the Impact on Children:

1. Emotional Reactions: Children may experience a range of emotions, including confusion, fear, sadness, and anger. They

may not understand why their parent is behaving differently or withdrawing emotionally.

2. Behavioral Changes: Changes in a parent's behavior can lead to changes in a child's behavior. Children may become more anxious, clingy, or exhibit regressive behaviors. Older children and adolescents may act out or become more withdrawn.

3. Sense of Responsibility: Some children may feel responsible for their parent's symptoms and try to take on a caregiving role. This can lead to increased stress and a sense of burden.

Strategies for Supporting Children:

1. Open Communication: Encourage open and age-appropriate communication about PTSD. Explain the condition in a way that children can understand and reassure them that they are not to blame for their parent's symptoms.

2. Provide Reassurance: Regularly reassure children of their safety and your love for them. Let them know that it is okay to have mixed feelings about the situation and that their emotions are valid.

3. Maintain Normalcy: Keep family routines and activities as normal as possible. Consistency and predictability provide a sense of security and stability for children.

4. Encourage Expression: Encourage children to express their feelings through talking, drawing, or other creative activities. Validate their emotions and provide a safe space for them to share their thoughts.

5. Model Healthy Coping: Demonstrate healthy coping strategies and self-care practices. Children learn by observing, and seeing a parent manage their symptoms can be reassuring.

6. Seek Professional Support: Consider involving a child therapist or counselor who can provide additional support and guidance for children. Professional support can help children

process their emotions and develop coping skills.

When Jake's PTSD symptoms worsened, his son, Sam, became more anxious and clingier. Jake and his wife decided to have an open conversation with Sam about PTSD, explaining that Jake's reactions were due to his condition and not because of anything Sam had done. They reassured Sam of their love and support and encouraged him to express his feelings through drawing. They also involved a child therapist who helped Sam understand and cope with his emotions. This approach helped Sam feel more secure and supported during a challenging time.

Supporting children when a parent has PTSD involves open communication, reassurance, and maintaining normalcy. By encouraging expression and seeking professional support, parents can help their children navigate the challenges and maintain their emotional well-being.

Building Resilience in Children

Building resilience in children is essential when a parent has PTSD. Resilience helps children adapt to challenges, cope with stress, and thrive despite difficult circumstances.

Key Components of Resilience:

1. Strong Relationships: Positive relationships with parents, caregivers, and other supportive adults provide children with a sense of security and belonging.

2. Emotional Awareness: Helping children recognize and understand their emotions is crucial for resilience. This includes validating their feelings and teaching them healthy ways to express and manage emotions.

3. Problem-Solving Skills: Encouraging children to develop problem-solving skills helps them feel capable and confident in handling challenges.

4. Self-Efficacy: Fostering a sense of self-efficacy involves

encouraging children to take on age-appropriate responsibilities and celebrate their successes.

5. Positive Outlook: Cultivating a positive outlook helps children see challenges as opportunities for growth. This includes encouraging optimism and a growth mindset.

Strategies for Building Resilience:

1. Foster Strong Connections: Encourage strong connections with family, friends, and community members. Positive relationships provide emotional support and a sense of belonging.

2. Encourage Emotional Expression: Create a safe environment for children to express their emotions. Validate their feelings and teach them healthy coping strategies, such as deep breathing, journaling, or talking to a trusted adult.

3. Promote Problem-Solving: Encourage children to solve problems independently by asking open-ended questions and guiding them through the decision-making process. Praise their efforts and solutions.

4. Set Realistic Goals: Help children set realistic and achievable goals. Break larger tasks into smaller, manageable steps and celebrate their accomplishments along the way.

5. Model Resilience: Demonstrate resilience through your actions and attitude. Show children how to handle setbacks with grace and perseverance.

6. Encourage a Positive Outlook: Foster a positive outlook by focusing on strengths, highlighting successes, and encouraging a growth mindset. Teach children to view challenges as opportunities for growth and learning.

After her husband was diagnosed with PTSD, Susan focused on building resilience in their two children. She encouraged open communication about their emotions and validated their feelings. Susan involved the children in setting small, achievable goals and celebrated their successes. She also modelled resilience by showing them how she managed stress and handled setbacks. Through these efforts, Susan helped her children develop the skills and confidence to navigate challenges and thrive.

Building resilience in children involves fostering strong relationships, promoting emotional awareness, and encouraging problem-solving skills. By modelling resilience and maintaining a positive outlook, parents can help their children develop the ability to adapt and thrive despite difficulties.

Family Therapy and Support

Family therapy and support can play a crucial role in helping families navigate the challenges of PTSD. Professional guidance can improve communication, strengthen relationships, and provide tools for managing symptoms collectively.

Benefits of Family Therapy:

1. Improved Communication: Family therapy facilitates open and honest communication among family members. It provides a safe space to express feelings, share experiences, and discuss concerns.

2. Strengthened Relationships: Therapy can help strengthen relationships by fostering understanding, empathy, and mutual support. It encourages family members to work together to overcome challenges.

3. Effective Coping Strategies: Therapists can teach families effective coping strategies to manage PTSD symptoms and reduce stress. These strategies can include relaxation techniques, conflict resolution skills, and stress management tools.

4. Increased Understanding: Family therapy helps family

members understand the impact of PTSD on their loved one and the family as a whole. It provides education about the condition and its symptoms, fostering empathy and support.

5. Building Resilience: Therapy can help families build resilience by developing problem-solving skills, setting goals, and creating a supportive environment.

Types of Family Support:

1. Family Therapy Sessions: Regular family therapy sessions with a licensed therapist can address specific issues and provide ongoing support. Sessions can be tailored to the family's needs and goals.

2. Support Groups: Joining support groups for families affected by PTSD can provide a sense of community and shared understanding. These groups offer a space to share experiences, gain insights, and receive emotional support.

3. Educational Workshops: Attending workshops or seminars on PTSD and family dynamics can provide valuable information and practical tools for managing symptoms and improving relationships.

4. Individual Therapy for Family Members: In addition to family therapy, individual therapy for family members can provide additional support. This allows each member to address their own feelings and challenges related to the family's experience with PTSD.

5. Community Resources: Accessing community resources, such as mental health organizations, parenting programs, and recreational activities, can provide additional support and opportunities for family bonding.

When Mark's PTSD symptoms began to affect his family, his wife, Lisa, suggested they attend family therapy. The therapist helped them improve communication and understand the impact of PTSD on their family dynamics. They learned effective coping strategies and developed a plan to support Mark's recovery while maintaining family harmony. Lisa and their children also attended a support group for families affected by PTSD, where they found additional support and understanding. Family therapy and support helped Mark and his family navigate the challenges together and strengthen their relationships.

Family therapy and support provide valuable tools and resources for families navigating PTSD. By improving communication, fostering understanding, and developing coping strategies, families can work together to manage symptoms and build resilience.

A Parent's Journey

After experiencing a traumatic event, Michelle struggled with PTSD while trying to care for her two young children. She often felt overwhelmed and disconnected, worrying that her symptoms were affecting her ability to be a good parent. Determined to find a way to manage her PTSD and be there for her children, Michelle embarked on a journey of self-discovery and healing.

Michelle began attending therapy to address her PTSD symptoms and learn coping strategies. Her therapist encouraged her to practice mindfulness exercises and self-care routines to manage her anxiety and stay present with her children. Michelle also worked on setting realistic expectations for herself and sought support from her family and friends.

To help her children understand what she was going through, Michelle had open and age-appropriate conversations with them about PTSD. She explained that her reactions were not their fault and reassured them of her love and commitment. Michelle encouraged her children to express their feelings and validated their emotions, creating a supportive and understanding environment at home.

Recognizing the importance of building resilience in her children, Michelle involved them in setting small goals and celebrated their achievements. She encouraged problem-solving and provided opportunities for them to take on age-appropriate responsibilities. Michelle also modelled healthy coping strategies, showing her children how to handle stress and setbacks with resilience.

Seeking additional support, Michelle and her family attended family therapy sessions. The therapist helped them improve communication, understand the impact of PTSD on their family dynamics, and develop effective coping strategies. Michelle's children also attended individual therapy, where they received guidance and support to process their emotions.

Through these efforts, Michelle found a balance between managing her PTSD and being a supportive parent. She realized that her journey was not about being a perfect parent but about being present and resilient for her children. Michelle's experience taught her that seeking help and building a support system were crucial for both her well-being and her family's.

Michelle's story highlights the challenges and triumphs of parenting with PTSD. By seeking therapy, practicing self-care, and fostering open communication, Michelle was able to navigate her journey with resilience and provide a supportive environment for her children.

A parent's journey with PTSD involves self-discovery, seeking support, and building resilience. By addressing their own needs and fostering a supportive family environment, parents can navigate the challenges of PTSD and create a positive impact on their children's lives.

CHAPTER 16: PTSD IN VETERANS

PTSD is a significant issue among veterans, many of whom have experienced intense and prolonged stress during their service. Understanding the nature of PTSD in veterans and the unique challenges they face is essential for providing effective support and promoting recovery.

Understanding PTSD in Veterans:

1. Causes and Risk Factors:

- Combat Exposure: Veterans often experience traumatic events such as combat, witnessing death, and life-threatening situations. These experiences can lead to the development of PTSD.

- Military Sexual Trauma (MST): MST, including sexual assault or harassment, is another risk factor for PTSD among veterans.

- Prolonged Stress: The prolonged stress and high-stakes environment of military service can contribute to the development of PTSD.

2. Common Symptoms:

- Re-Experiencing: Veterans may experience flashbacks, nightmares, and intrusive thoughts about their traumatic experiences.

- Avoidance: Avoiding reminders of the trauma, including people, places, and activities, is a common symptom.

- Hyperarousal: Veterans may be hypervigilant, easily startled, and experience difficulty sleeping and concentrating.

 - Negative Changes in Mood and Cognition: Feelings of guilt, shame, and depression, along with negative beliefs about oneself and the world, are common.

3. Impact on Daily Life:

 - Relationships: PTSD can strain relationships with family, friends, and colleagues due to emotional numbing, irritability, and withdrawal.

 - Employment: Symptoms of PTSD can affect job performance, leading to difficulties in maintaining employment or transitioning to civilian work.

 - Physical Health: PTSD is often associated with physical health issues such as chronic pain, cardiovascular problems, and substance abuse.

After serving in combat, John struggled with PTSD. He experienced frequent flashbacks and nightmares, which made it difficult for him to sleep and function during the day. John avoided social situations and felt disconnected from his family. Understanding that his symptoms were a result of PTSD helped John seek the appropriate support and begin his journey to recovery.

Understanding PTSD in veterans involves recognizing the causes, symptoms, and impact on daily life. By acknowledging these factors, we can better support veterans in their recovery and help them lead fulfilling lives.

Unique Challenges Faced by Veterans

Veterans with PTSD face unique challenges that can complicate their recovery and reintegration into civilian life. Addressing these challenges requires tailored approaches and support systems.

Challenges Faced by Veterans:

1. Transition to Civilian Life:

- Loss of Identity and Purpose: Many veterans struggle with the transition from military to civilian life. The military often provides a strong sense of identity and purpose, which can be lost upon discharge.
- Cultural Adjustment: Adjusting to civilian culture, which may have different values and expectations, can be challenging for veterans.

2. Stigma and Barriers to Care:
- Stigma: There is often a stigma associated with mental health issues in the military, which can prevent veterans from seeking help.
- Access to Care: Veterans may face barriers to accessing mental health care, including long wait times, limited availability of specialized services, and geographic challenges.

3. Co-Occurring Conditions:
- Substance Use Disorders: Many veterans with PTSD also struggle with substance use disorders, which can complicate treatment and recovery.
- Physical Health Issues: Chronic pain, traumatic brain injury (TBI), and other physical health issues are common among veterans and can impact mental health.

4. Isolation and Relationship Strains:
- Social Isolation: Veterans may feel isolated from civilian society and experience difficulties connecting with others who do not share their experiences.
- Relationship Strains: PTSD can strain relationships with family and friends, leading to further isolation and emotional difficulties.

5. Employment and Financial Stability:
- Employment Challenges: Veterans with PTSD may face difficulties in finding and maintaining employment due to their symptoms and the need for a supportive work environment.
- Financial Strain: Unemployment or underemployment can

lead to financial strain, adding additional stress to veterans' lives.

Addressing the Challenges:

1. Tailored Mental Health Services: Providing specialized mental health services that address the unique needs of veterans can improve access to care and treatment outcomes.

2. Veteran Support Programs: Programs that focus on supporting veterans' transition to civilian life, including job training, education, and financial assistance, can help ease the transition.

3. Peer Support: Peer support groups and programs can provide veterans with a sense of community and understanding, reducing feelings of isolation.

4. Integrated Care: Integrating mental health and physical health care can address co-occurring conditions and provide comprehensive support.

5. Stigma Reduction: Efforts to reduce stigma around mental health in the military and veteran communities can encourage more veterans to seek help.

After leaving the military, Lisa struggled with the transition to civilian life. She felt isolated and had difficulty finding employment. Lisa also faced barriers to accessing mental health care due to long wait times at the VA. With the support of a veteran peer group and specialized mental health services, Lisa was able to find a sense of community and begin her journey to recovery. Addressing the unique challenges faced by veterans is essential for supporting their recovery and reintegration into civilian life.

Veterans with PTSD face unique challenges that require tailored approaches and support systems. By addressing these challenges, we can provide the necessary support to help veterans lead fulfilling lives and successfully transition to civilian life.

Support Systems for Veterans

Effective support systems are crucial for helping veterans with PTSD manage their symptoms and improve their quality of life. These systems include a combination of medical, psychological, and community-based support.

Medical and Psychological Support:

1. Veterans Affairs (VA) Services: The VA provides comprehensive health care services for veterans, including mental health care, medical treatment, and support for substance use disorders. Accessing VA services can provide veterans with specialized care tailored to their needs.

2. Therapy and Counseling: Various forms of therapy, such as Cognitive Behavioral Therapy (CBT), Eye Movement Desensitization and Reprocessing (EMDR), and Prolonged Exposure Therapy, are effective in treating PTSD. Veterans can access these therapies through the VA or private providers.

3. Medication Management: Medications such as antidepressants and anti-anxiety medications can help manage PTSD symptoms. A healthcare provider can work with veterans to find the right medication and dosage.

4. Integrated Care Programs: Programs that integrate mental health and physical health care can address co-occurring conditions and provide comprehensive support. These programs can help manage chronic pain, TBI, and other health issues alongside PTSD treatment.

Community and Peer Support:

1. Veteran Peer Support Groups: Peer support groups provide a space for veterans to share their experiences and receive support from others who understand their challenges. These

groups can be found through the VA, veteran organizations, and community centers.

2. Veteran Service Organizations: Organizations such as the American Legion, Veterans of Foreign Wars (VFW), and Iraq and Afghanistan Veterans of America (IAVA) offer various forms of support, including advocacy, financial assistance, and community events.

3. Family and Friends: Support from family and friends is crucial for veterans' recovery. Providing education about PTSD and involving loved ones in treatment can strengthen support networks and improve outcomes.

4. Employment and Education Programs: Programs that offer job training, education, and employment support can help veterans transition to civilian careers and achieve financial stability. These programs can also provide a sense of purpose and fulfillment.

5. Recreational and Therapeutic Activities: Engaging in recreational activities, such as sports, art, and outdoor adventures, can provide therapeutic benefits and improve mental health. Programs like adaptive sports and therapeutic horseback riding can be particularly beneficial.

After struggling with PTSD and feeling isolated, Tom joined a veteran peer support group through the VA. The group provided him with a sense of community and understanding. Tom also accessed therapy and medication management through the VA, which helped him manage his symptoms. Additionally, he participated in an adaptive sports program, which improved his physical health and provided a positive outlet for stress. The combination of medical, psychological, and community support systems helped Tom find stability and improve his quality of life.

Support systems for veterans with PTSD include medical and psychological care, community and peer support, and programs for employment and education. By accessing these resources, veterans can receive comprehensive support and improve their overall well-being.

Success Stories of Veteran Recovery

Hearing success stories of veteran recovery can provide hope and inspiration to those struggling with PTSD. These stories demonstrate that with the right support and determination, it is possible to overcome challenges and lead fulfilling lives.

Success Story 1: James' Journey to Recovery

James, a combat veteran, struggled with severe PTSD after returning from deployment. He experienced flashbacks, nightmares, and intense anxiety, which made it difficult for him to function in daily life. James decided to seek help and enrolled in a comprehensive treatment program through the VA.

Through a combination of therapy, medication management, and support from a veteran peer group, James began to see improvements in his symptoms. He participated in Cognitive Behavioral Therapy (CBT) and found that it helped him process his traumatic experiences and develop healthier coping mechanisms.

James also joined an adaptive sports program, where he discovered a passion for cycling. The physical activity and sense of accomplishment from participating in races provided a positive outlet for his energy and stress. With the support of his family and friends, James continued to make progress and eventually found stability in his life.

Success Story 2: Lisa's Path to Healing

Lisa, a veteran who experienced military sexual trauma (MST), struggled with PTSD and depression

. She felt isolated and hesitant to seek help due to the stigma surrounding mental health. Encouraged by a fellow veteran,

Lisa decided to reach out to a therapist who specialized in treating MST.

Through therapy, Lisa learned to process her trauma and rebuild her sense of self-worth. She also participated in group therapy sessions with other survivors, which provided a supportive and understanding community. Lisa found solace in art therapy, where she could express her emotions creatively.

In addition to therapy, Lisa joined a local veteran service organization that offered job training and employment support. She pursued a new career in social work, inspired by her desire to help others who had experienced similar challenges. Lisa's journey to healing was marked by determination and the support of a strong network.

Success Story 3: Tom's New Beginning

Tom, a veteran with PTSD, faced significant challenges in transitioning to civilian life. He struggled with finding stable employment and managing his symptoms. Feeling discouraged, Tom reached out to a veteran support organization that offered comprehensive services for veterans.

Tom participated in a vocational training program that helped him develop new skills and find a job that suited his interests. He also accessed mental health services through the organization, including therapy and medication management. The combination of career support and mental health care helped Tom regain his confidence and stability.

Tom found additional support through a veteran peer group, where he connected with others who shared similar experiences. The sense of camaraderie and understanding provided by the group was instrumental in his recovery. Tom's new beginning was characterized by resilience and the support of a strong network.

Success stories of veteran recovery highlight the importance of comprehensive support and determination. By accessing therapy, community resources, and support from peers and loved ones, veterans can overcome challenges and lead fulfilling lives.

A Veteran's Triumph

After serving in the military for over a decade, Mark returned home with severe PTSD. The transition to civilian life was difficult, and he struggled with flashbacks, hypervigilance, and anxiety. Mark felt disconnected from his family and friends and found it challenging to hold down a job. His symptoms left him feeling hopeless and isolated.

Determined to reclaim his life, Mark decided to seek help through the VA. He enrolled in a comprehensive PTSD treatment program that included individual therapy, group therapy, and medication management. Mark participated in Cognitive Processing Therapy (CPT), which helped him process his traumatic memories and reduce the intensity of his symptoms.

In addition to therapy, Mark joined a veteran peer support group. The group provided a safe space for him to share his experiences and receive support from others who understood his struggles. The camaraderie and understanding he found in the group were instrumental in his recovery.

Mark also explored new hobbies and activities that brought him joy and relaxation. He discovered a passion for woodworking and found that creating furniture and art pieces helped him stay focused and grounded. The sense of accomplishment he gained from his woodworking projects boosted his confidence and provided a positive outlet for his energy.

With the support of his family, Mark worked on rebuilding his relationships. He practiced open communication and involved his loved ones in his recovery journey. Mark's wife and children attended family therapy sessions with him, which helped them understand PTSD and learn how to support him effectively.

Over time, Mark's symptoms became more manageable, and he found stability in his life. He secured a job that he enjoyed and felt proud of his accomplishments. Mark's journey to recovery was marked by resilience, determination, and the unwavering support of his family and community.

Mark's story is a testament to the strength and resilience of veterans with PTSD. By seeking help, accessing comprehensive support, and finding new passions, Mark was able to overcome his challenges and lead a fulfilling life. His triumph serves as an inspiration to other veterans who are navigating their own recovery journeys.

A veteran's triumph over PTSD involves seeking help, building a support network, and finding new passions. By accessing comprehensive care and maintaining determination, veterans can overcome their challenges and lead fulfilling lives.

CHAPTER 17: PTSD IN FIRST RESPONDERS

First responders, including police officers, firefighters, paramedics, and emergency medical technicians, frequently encounter traumatic events as part of their duties. The constant exposure to trauma can significantly impact their mental health, leading to PTSD.

The Impact of Trauma on First Responders:

1. Exposure to Traumatic Events:
   - First responders often witness distressing scenes, such as accidents, natural disasters, violence, and death. This repeated exposure can lead to the development of PTSD.

2. Cumulative Stress:
   - The cumulative stress of dealing with multiple traumatic incidents over time can have a profound impact on mental health. Even if a single event might not cause PTSD, the accumulation of stress can.

3. High-Pressure Environment:
   - First responders work in high-pressure environments where they must make quick decisions and provide critical care. This constant state of alertness can contribute to chronic stress and anxiety.

4. Emotional Toll:
   - The emotional toll of witnessing suffering and loss can lead

to feelings of helplessness, guilt, and sadness. This emotional burden can be difficult to process and manage.

5. Impact on Personal Life:
   - The stress and trauma experienced by first responders can spill over into their personal lives, affecting relationships, sleep, and overall well-being.

Common Symptoms of PTSD in First Responders:

1. Re-Experiencing:
   - Flashbacks, nightmares, and intrusive thoughts about traumatic events are common symptoms. These re-experiencing symptoms can be triggered by reminders of the trauma.

2. Avoidance:
   - Avoiding people, places, or activities that are reminders of the trauma is a common coping mechanism. This can lead to isolation and withdrawal from social and professional activities.

3. Hyperarousal:
   - Symptoms of hyperarousal include being easily startled, feeling tense or on edge, and having difficulty sleeping. These symptoms can impact job performance and personal life.

4. Negative Changes in Mood and Cognition:
   - Feelings of guilt, shame, and hopelessness, along with negative beliefs about oneself and the world, can affect mental health. These changes can lead to depression and anxiety.

After years of working as a paramedic, David began to experience severe anxiety and flashbacks. The constant exposure to traumatic scenes took a toll on his mental health. David found it difficult to sleep and often felt on edge. Recognizing the impact of his work on his mental health, David sought help and began his journey to recovery.

The impact of trauma on first responders is significant, affecting their mental health and overall well-being. Understanding the common symptoms of PTSD and recognizing the emotional toll is crucial for providing the necessary support and resources.

Recognizing PTSD in First Responders

Early recognition of PTSD symptoms in first responders is crucial for timely intervention and effective treatment. Understanding the signs and symptoms can help identify those in need of support.

Signs and Symptoms of PTSD:

1. Behavioral Changes:
   - Noticeable changes in behavior, such as increased irritability, anger outbursts, or withdrawal from social activities, can be indicators of PTSD. First responders may also exhibit changes in work performance or attendance.
2. Emotional Symptoms:
   - Persistent feelings of sadness, guilt, or hopelessness, along with emotional numbness or detachment, can signal PTSD. First responders may also experience intense fear or anxiety.

3. Cognitive Symptoms:
   - Difficulty concentrating, memory problems, and negative thoughts about oneself or the world are common cognitive symptoms. First responders may also experience confusion or difficulty making decisions.

4. Physical Symptoms:
   - Physical symptoms such as headaches, gastrointestinal issues, and chronic pain can be associated with PTSD. Sleep disturbances, including insomnia and nightmares, are also common.

5. Re-Experiencing Symptoms:
   - Flashbacks, nightmares, and intrusive thoughts about traumatic events are hallmark symptoms of PTSD. These re-experiencing symptoms can be triggered by reminders of the

trauma.

6. Avoidance Symptoms:

- Avoiding reminders of the traumatic event, such as people, places, or activities, is a common coping mechanism. This avoidance can lead to isolation and withdrawal.

Barriers to Recognizing PTSD:

1. Stigma:

- The stigma associated with mental health issues can prevent first responders from seeking help. Fear of being perceived as weak or unfit for duty can lead to reluctance in acknowledging symptoms.

2. Cultural Norms:

- The culture within first responder communities often values toughness and resilience. This can create pressure to suppress emotions and avoid discussing mental health issues.

3. Lack of Awareness:

- Lack of awareness about PTSD and its symptoms can delay recognition and intervention. First responders and their colleagues may not be familiar with the signs of PTSD.

4. Occupational Factors:

- The demanding nature of the job can make it difficult for first responders to find time to seek help. Shift work, long hours, and constant exposure to trauma can exacerbate symptoms.

Strategies for Early Recognition:

1. Education and Training:

- Providing education and training on PTSD for first responders and their supervisors can increase awareness and promote early recognition. This includes training on the signs and symptoms of PTSD and how to seek help.

2. Peer Support Programs:

- Implementing peer support programs can provide first

responders with a safe space to discuss their experiences and seek support. Peers who understand the challenges of the job can offer valuable insights and encouragement.

3. Regular Mental Health Screenings:
   - Conducting regular mental health screenings for first responders can help identify those at risk for PTSD. These screenings can be integrated into routine medical evaluations.

4. Encouraging Open Communication:
   - Promoting a culture of open communication within first responder communities can reduce stigma and encourage individuals to seek help. Leadership should model and support open discussions about mental health.

Sarah, a firefighter, noticed changes in her behavior and emotions after responding to a particularly traumatic fire. She began avoiding social activities and felt increasingly anxious. Sarah's department had implemented regular mental health screenings, and during one of these evaluations, she was identified as being at risk for PTSD. With the support of her peers and supervisors, Sarah sought treatment and began her journey to recovery.

Recognizing PTSD in first responders involves understanding the signs and symptoms and addressing the barriers to seeking help. Through education, peer support, and regular screenings, early recognition and intervention can be achieved.

Specialized Support and Resources

Providing specialized support and resources for first responders with PTSD is essential for their recovery and well-being. Tailored programs and services can address their unique needs and promote resilience.

Specialized Support for First Responders:

1. Trauma-Informed Therapy:

- Trauma-informed therapy, such as Cognitive Behavioral Therapy (CBT), Eye Movement Desensitization and Reprocessing (EMDR), and Prolonged Exposure Therapy, can help first responders process traumatic experiences and reduce symptoms.

2. Peer Support Programs:
   - Peer support programs connect first responders with colleagues who have experienced similar challenges. These programs provide a safe space for sharing experiences, receiving support, and building resilience.

3. Critical Incident Stress Management (CISM):
   - CISM programs offer structured support following traumatic incidents. These programs include debriefing sessions, counseling, and stress management techniques to help first responders cope with acute stress reactions.

4. Employee Assistance Programs (EAP):
   - EAPs provide confidential counseling and support services for first responders and their families. These programs offer access to mental health professionals and resources to address various issues, including PTSD.

5. Resilience Training:
   - Resilience training programs teach first responders skills to manage stress, build emotional resilience, and maintain mental health. These programs often include mindfulness, relaxation techniques, and stress reduction strategies.

6. Veteran Support Organizations:
   - Organizations like the Firefighter Behavioral Health Alliance (FBHA) and the Code Green Campaign provide specialized support for first responders. These organizations offer resources, advocacy, and programs tailored to the needs of first responders.

Resources for First Responders:

1. Hotlines and Crisis Support:
   - Hotlines such as the National Suicide Prevention Lifeline and the Crisis Text Line offer immediate support for first responders in crisis. These services provide confidential help and can connect individuals to further resources.

2. Online Resources and Communities:
   - Websites and online forums dedicated to first responder mental health offer information, support, and a sense of community. These platforms provide access to educational materials, self-help tools, and peer support.

3. Workshops and Training:
   - Workshops and training sessions focused on mental health and resilience can provide valuable skills and knowledge. These programs can be offered through professional organizations, mental health agencies, or first responder departments.

4. Mental Health Apps:
   - Mobile apps designed for mental health support can provide first responders with tools for managing stress, tracking symptoms, and accessing resources. Apps like Headspace, PTSD Coach, and Mindfulness Coach can be useful tools.

5. Family Support Services:
   - Support services for families of first responders can help loved ones understand PTSD and provide effective support. Family counseling, support groups, and educational resources can strengthen family resilience.

After experiencing several traumatic incidents as a police officer, Mike began to struggle with PTSD. He felt isolated and unsure where to turn for help. Mike's department had a peer support program, and through it, he connected with colleagues who had faced similar challenges. They encouraged him to seek trauma-informed therapy and provided ongoing support. Mike also accessed resources from a veteran support organization, which offered resilience training and online support. These specialized programs and resources were instrumental in his recovery journey.

Specialized support and resources for first responders with PTSD include trauma-informed therapy, peer support, and resilience training. By accessing these tailored programs and services, first responders can receive the help they need to manage their symptoms and maintain their mental health.

Success Stories of First Responder Recovery

Success stories of first responder recovery can provide hope and inspiration to those struggling with PTSD. These stories highlight the resilience and determination of individuals who have overcome significant challenges.

Success Story 1: Emily's Path to Healing

Emily, a paramedic, began experiencing severe PTSD symptoms after responding to a series of traumatic calls. She struggled with flashbacks, nightmares, and anxiety, which affected her ability to work and her relationships. Emily decided to seek help through her department's Employee Assistance Program (EAP).

Through the EAP, Emily accessed trauma-informed therapy, including EMDR and Cognitive Behavioral Therapy (CBT). She also joined a peer support group for first responders, where she found understanding and encouragement from colleagues who shared similar experiences. Emily participated in resilience training workshops that taught her stress management techniques and mindfulness practices.

Over time, Emily's symptoms began to improve. She felt more in control of her emotions and more connected to her work and relationships. Emily's path to healing was marked by her commitment to seeking help and the support of specialized programs.

Success Story 2: Mark's Journey to Recovery

Mark, a firefighter, experienced PTSD after responding to a particularly devastating fire. He felt overwhelmed by flashbacks and hypervigilance, which made it difficult for him to perform his duties. Mark's supervisor recognized the signs of PTSD and encouraged him to seek help.

Mark enrolled in a Critical Incident Stress Management (CISM) program, which provided immediate support and counseling following the traumatic incident. He also accessed therapy through a local mental health organization that specialized in treating first responders. Mark joined a veteran support organization, where he participated in workshops on resilience and coping strategies.

With the support of his supervisor, peers, and specialized programs, Mark made significant progress in his recovery. He learned effective coping mechanisms and rebuilt his confidence in his abilities as a firefighter. Mark's journey to recovery was a testament to the importance of early intervention and comprehensive support.

Success Story 3: Sarah's Resilience

Sarah, a police officer, struggled with PTSD after witnessing a traumatic event while on duty. She experienced severe anxiety and emotional numbness, which impacted her work and personal life. Sarah felt isolated and hesitant to seek help due to the stigma surrounding mental health.

Encouraged by a colleague, Sarah reached out to a trauma-informed therapist who specialized in treating first responders. She engaged in Prolonged Exposure Therapy and found it helpful in processing her traumatic experiences. Sarah also joined an online support community for first responders, where she found solace and understanding.

Sarah participated in resilience training programs that taught her mindfulness and relaxation techniques. She also involved her family in her recovery journey by attending family counseling sessions. With the support of her therapist, colleagues, and family, Sarah developed the resilience to manage her symptoms and continue her career.

Success stories of first responder recovery highlight the importance of seeking help, accessing specialized support, and building resilience. These stories demonstrate that with determination and the right resources, first responders can overcome PTSD and thrive.

A First Responder's Resilience

After serving as a paramedic for over a decade, John began to experience severe PTSD symptoms following a particularly traumatic call. He struggled with flashbacks, nightmares, and intense anxiety, which made it difficult for him to continue working. John felt isolated and unsure of where to turn for help.

Determined to regain control of his life, John reached out to his department's Employee Assistance Program (EAP). Through the EAP, he accessed trauma-informed therapy, including Cognitive Behavioral Therapy (CBT) and Eye Movement Desensitization and Reprocessing (EMDR). These therapies helped John process his traumatic experiences and develop healthier coping mechanisms.

In addition to therapy, John joined a peer support group for first responders. The group provided a safe space for him to share his experiences and receive support from colleagues who understood his struggles. The camaraderie and understanding he found in the group were instrumental in his recovery.

John also participated in resilience training workshops that taught him stress management techniques, mindfulness practices, and relaxation exercises. These skills helped him manage his symptoms and maintain his mental health. John found that regular exercise, a healthy diet, and sufficient sleep were crucial components of his self-care routine.

To further support his recovery, John connected with a veteran support organization that offered additional resources and programs for first responders. He attended workshops on resilience, stress reduction, and mental health advocacy. The organization also provided online resources and a sense of community.

With the support of his therapist, peers, and specialized programs, John made significant progress in his recovery. He felt more in control of his emotions, more connected to his work, and more confident in his ability to manage his symptoms. John's resilience and determination were key factors in his journey to recovery.

John's story is a testament to the strength and resilience of first responders with PTSD. By seeking help, accessing comprehensive support, and developing healthy coping mechanisms, John was able to overcome his challenges and continue his career. His experience serves as an inspiration to other first responders who are navigating their own recovery journeys.

A first responder's resilience involves seeking help, building a support network, and developing healthy coping mechanisms. By accessing specialized support and maintaining determination, first responders can overcome PTSD and thrive in their professional and personal lives.

CHAPTER 18: PTSD IN CHILDREN AND ADOLESCENTS

Children and adolescents are not immune to the effects of trauma. PTSD can significantly impact younger populations, affecting their development, behavior, and overall well-being. Understanding PTSD in children and adolescents is crucial for providing effective support and treatment.

Understanding PTSD in Younger Populations:

1. Causes of PTSD in Children and Adolescents:
   - Traumatic Events: Exposure to traumatic events such as physical or sexual abuse, domestic violence, natural disasters, serious accidents, and loss of a loved one can lead to PTSD.
   - Chronic Stress: Ongoing exposure to stressful environments, such as living in a war zone or experiencing prolonged neglect, can also contribute to the development of PTSD.
   - Witnessing Trauma: Even if children are not directly involved, witnessing traumatic events, such as violence or accidents, can result in PTSD.

2. Developmental Impact:
   - Emotional Development: Trauma can disrupt emotional development, leading to difficulties in regulating emotions, increased anxiety, and depression.
   - Behavioral Changes: Children and adolescents with PTSD

may exhibit changes in behavior, such as increased aggression, withdrawal, or difficulty concentrating.

- Cognitive Development: PTSD can impact cognitive development, affecting memory, attention, and learning. It can also lead to negative beliefs about oneself and the world.

3. Unique Aspects of PTSD in Children:

- Different Symptom Presentation: PTSD symptoms in children can differ from those in adults. For example, younger children may display symptoms through play or drawings, while adolescents may engage in risky behaviors.

- Influence of Developmental Stage: The impact of trauma can vary depending on the child's developmental stage. Younger children may have more difficulty understanding and verbalizing their experiences, while adolescents may struggle with identity and peer relationships.

After witnessing a car accident, eight-year-old Emma began experiencing nightmares and severe anxiety. She became fearful of leaving the house and had difficulty concentrating in school. Emma's parents noticed these changes and sought help from a child psychologist. Through therapy, Emma was able to process her trauma and learn coping strategies to manage her symptoms.

Understanding PTSD in children and adolescents involves recognizing the causes, developmental impact, and unique aspects of symptoms in younger populations. Early intervention and tailored support are essential for promoting recovery and well-being.

Recognizing Symptoms in Children and Teens

Recognizing the symptoms of PTSD in children and adolescents is essential for timely intervention and support. Symptoms can manifest differently in younger populations compared to adults.

Symptoms of PTSD in Children:

1. Re-Experiencing Symptoms:
   - Nightmares and Sleep Disturbances: Children with PTSD may experience frequent nightmares or difficulty sleeping.
   - Flashbacks and Intrusive Thoughts: They may have flashbacks or intrusive thoughts about the traumatic event.
   - Reenactment Through Play: Younger children may reenact the traumatic event through play or drawings.

2. Avoidance Symptoms:
   - Avoiding Reminders: Children may avoid people, places, or activities that remind them of the trauma.
   - Emotional Numbing: They may become emotionally numb or detached from their surroundings and loved ones.

3. Hyperarousal Symptoms:
   - Irritability and Anger: Increased irritability, anger outbursts, and frustration are common.
   - Hypervigilance: Children may be overly alert and easily startled.
   - Difficulty Concentrating: They may have trouble focusing on tasks or activities.

4. Negative Changes in Mood and Cognition:
   - Feelings of Guilt or Shame: Children may feel guilty or blame themselves for the traumatic event.
   - Negative Beliefs: They may develop negative beliefs about themselves, others, or the world.
   - Loss of Interest: Children may lose interest in activities they once enjoyed.

Symptoms of PTSD in Adolescents:

1. Re-Experiencing Symptoms:
   - Flashbacks and Intrusive Thoughts: Similar to children, adolescents may experience flashbacks and intrusive thoughts about the trauma.
   - Distressing Memories: Persistent, distressing memories of

the traumatic event are common.

2. Avoidance Symptoms:
- Avoiding Reminders: Adolescents may avoid situations, people, or places that remind them of the trauma.
- Withdrawal: They may withdraw from friends and family and lose interest in social activities.

3. Hyperarousal Symptoms:
- Irritability and Anger: Increased irritability and anger outbursts are common in adolescents with PTSD.
- Hypervigilance: Adolescents may be constantly on guard and easily startled.
- Sleep Disturbances: Difficulty sleeping, and frequent nightmares are common.

4. Negative Changes in Mood and Cognition:
- Feelings of Hopelessness: Adolescents may feel hopeless about the future.
- Negative Self-Perception: They may develop a negative self-image and feelings of worthlessness.
- Risky Behaviors: Adolescents may engage in risky behaviors, such as substance use or self-harm, as a way to cope with their emotions.

Early Recognition and Intervention:

1. Observation and Communication: Parents, caregivers, and educators should observe changes in behavior and emotional responses. Open communication with children and adolescents about their feelings and experiences is crucial.

2. Seeking Professional Help: Early intervention by mental health professionals can provide children and adolescents with the necessary support and treatment. Therapists can help them process their trauma and develop healthy coping strategies.

3. Education and Awareness: Educating parents, teachers, and caregivers about the signs and symptoms of PTSD in

children and adolescents can promote early recognition and intervention.

After experiencing a traumatic event, 15-year-old Alex began to withdraw from friends and family. He had frequent nightmares and became increasingly irritable. Alex's parents noticed these changes and sought help from a therapist who specialized in adolescent trauma. Through therapy, Alex was able to process his trauma and develop healthier coping mechanisms, leading to significant improvements in his mental health.

Recognizing the symptoms of PTSD in children and adolescents involves observing changes in behavior and emotional responses. Early recognition and intervention are crucial for providing timely support and promoting recovery.

Effective Treatments for Young People

Effective treatments for PTSD in children and adolescents are tailored to their developmental stage and individual needs. These treatments can help young people process their trauma, develop healthy coping strategies, and improve their overall well-being.

Therapeutic Approaches:

1. Trauma-Focused Cognitive Behavioral Therapy (TF-CBT):
   - Overview: TF-CBT is a structured, evidence-based treatment that helps children and adolescents process traumatic experiences and develop coping skills.
   - Components: The therapy includes psychoeducation, relaxation techniques, cognitive processing, and exposure to trauma-related memories.
   - Effectiveness: TF-CBT has been shown to reduce PTSD symptoms, anxiety, and depression in children and adolescents.

2. Play Therapy:
   - Overview: Play therapy uses play as a medium for children to express their emotions and process traumatic experiences.

- Techniques: Techniques include using toys, games, and creative activities to help children communicate their feelings and work through trauma.

- Effectiveness: Play therapy is particularly effective for younger children who may have difficulty verbalizing their experiences.

3. Eye Movement Desensitization and Reprocessing (EMDR):

- Overview: EMDR is a structured therapy that uses bilateral stimulation (such as eye movements) to help individuals process traumatic memories.

- Application: EMDR can be adapted for children and adolescents, helping them reduce the distress associated with traumatic memories.

- Effectiveness: EMDR has been shown to be effective in reducing PTSD symptoms in young people.

4. Dialectical Behavior Therapy (DBT):

- Overview: DBT is a cognitive-behavioral treatment that focuses on teaching skills for emotional regulation, distress tolerance, and interpersonal effectiveness.

- Application: DBT can be adapted for adolescents with PTSD, helping them manage intense emotions and reduce self-destructive behaviors.

- Effectiveness: DBT has been shown to improve emotional regulation and reduce PTSD symptoms in adolescents.

5. Narrative Exposure Therapy (NET):

- Overview: NET is a therapeutic approach that involves creating a detailed narrative of the traumatic experience to help individuals process and integrate the trauma.

- Application: NET can be used with children and adolescents to help them make sense of their experiences and reduce PTSD symptoms.

- Effectiveness: NET has been shown to be effective in reducing PTSD symptoms and improving overall functioning.

Supportive Interventions:

1. Family Therapy:
   - Overview: Family therapy involves the entire family in the treatment process, helping to improve communication, support, and understanding.
   - Benefits: It can address family dynamics and provide support to both the child and their family members.
   - Effectiveness: Family therapy can improve the overall functioning and well-being of the child and their family.

2. Group Therapy:
   - Overview: Group therapy provides a supportive environment where children and adolescents can share their experiences and learn from others.
   - Benefits: It fosters a sense of community and reduces feelings of isolation.
   - Effectiveness: Group therapy can be an effective adjunct to individual therapy, providing additional support and coping strategies.

3. School-Based Interventions:
   - Overview: School-based interventions provide support within the educational setting, helping children and adolescents manage their symptoms and succeed academically.
   - Components: Interventions can include counseling, psychoeducation, and accommodations for academic and behavioral challenges.
   - Effectiveness: School-based interventions can improve academic performance and reduce PTSD symptoms.

After experiencing a traumatic event, 12-year-old Mia struggled with anxiety and flashbacks. Her parents sought help from a therapist who specialized in TF-CBT. Through therapy, Mia learned relaxation techniques, processed her traumatic memories, and developed healthier coping mechanisms. Additionally, Mia's school provided counseling support, which helped her manage her symptoms and succeed academically. The combination of TF-CBT and school-based interventions significantly improved Mia's mental health and well-being.

Effective treatments for PTSD in children and adolescents include trauma-focused cognitive behavioral therapy, play therapy, EMDR, DBT, and NET. Supportive interventions such as family therapy, group therapy, and school-based interventions can further enhance the recovery process.

Support Systems for Children and Adolescents

A strong support system is crucial for the recovery of children and adolescents with PTSD. These support systems can include family, peers, schools, and community resources, all working together to provide comprehensive care.

Family Support:

1. Parental Involvement:
   - Communication: Open and honest communication between parents and children is essential. Parents should listen to their child's concerns and validate their feelings.
   - Education: Parents should educate themselves about PTSD and its impact on children. Understanding the condition can help them provide better support.
   - Consistency: Maintaining consistent routines and providing a stable environment can help children feel safe and secure.

2. Family Therapy:
   - Involvement: Involving the entire family in therapy can improve communication, address family dynamics, and provide support to both the child and family members.
   - Benefits: Family therapy can help the family understand the child's experiences and develop strategies to support their recovery.

School Support:

1. Counseling Services:
   - Availability: Schools should provide access to counseling services for students experiencing PTSD symptoms. School counselors can offer individual and group therapy.
   - Support: Counselors can help students manage their symptoms, develop coping strategies, and succeed academically.

2. Educational Accommodations:
   - Flexibility: Schools should offer accommodations to support students with PTSD, such as extended time for assignments, modified workloads, and a quiet space for breaks.
   - Collaboration: Teachers, counselors, and parents should collaborate to create an individualized education plan (IEP) that addresses the student's needs.

Peer Support:

1. Peer Support Groups:
   - Group Dynamics: Peer support groups provide a safe space for children and adolescents to share their experiences and receive support from others who understand their struggles.
   - Benefits: These groups can reduce feelings of isolation and promote a sense of community and belonging.

2. Peer Mentoring Programs:
   - Mentorship: Peer mentoring programs pair younger children with older peers who have experienced similar challenges. Mentors can offer guidance, support, and encouragement.
   - Impact: Peer mentoring can foster positive relationships and provide role models for children and adolescents.

Community Resources:

1. Mental Health Services:
   - Access: Community mental health centers can provide access to specialized therapists and programs for children and adolescents with PTSD.
   - Support: These centers often offer a range of services,

including individual therapy, group therapy, and family counseling.

2. Recreational Programs:
- Activities: Community centers and organizations may offer recreational programs, such as sports, arts, and outdoor activities, that provide therapeutic benefits and promote social connections.
- Benefits: Engaging in recreational activities can improve mental health, build confidence, and reduce stress.

3. Support for Caregivers:
- Resources: Caregivers should have access to resources and support groups that provide education, emotional support, and practical strategies for managing their child's PTSD.
- Importance: Supporting caregivers helps them provide better care for their children and reduces caregiver stress.

After experiencing a traumatic event, 10-year-old Jake began to struggle with anxiety and avoidance behaviors. His parents sought help from a local mental health center, where Jake received individual therapy and the family participated in family counseling sessions. Jake's school provided counseling services and academic accommodations to support his learning needs. Additionally, Jake joined a peer support group, where he connected with other children who had similar experiences. The combination of family support, school support, peer support, and community resources helped Jake manage his symptoms and improve his overall well-being.

A strong support system for children and adolescents with PTSD includes family involvement, school support, peer support, and community resources. By working together, these systems can provide comprehensive care and promote recovery.

A Young Survivor's Journey

At the age of 14, Rachel experienced a traumatic event that left her struggling with severe PTSD. She had frequent flashbacks, nightmares, and intense anxiety, which affected her ability to attend school and interact with friends. Rachel felt isolated and overwhelmed by her emotions.

Recognizing the impact of the trauma on Rachel's well-being, her parents sought help from a child psychologist who specialized in trauma. Rachel began trauma-focused cognitive behavioral therapy (TF-CBT), where she learned to process her traumatic memories and develop healthy coping strategies. Her therapist helped her understand that her symptoms were a normal response to trauma and that recovery was possible.

In addition to individual therapy, Rachel's school provided support through counseling services and academic accommodations. Her school counselor worked with her teachers to create an individualized education plan (IEP) that addressed her needs. This plan included extended time for assignments, a quiet space for breaks, and flexibility in her schedule.

Rachel also joined a peer support group for adolescents who had experienced trauma. The group provided a safe space for Rachel to share her experiences and receive support from others who understood her struggles. She found comfort in knowing she was not alone and formed meaningful connections with her peers.

To further support her recovery, Rachel participated in art therapy, which allowed her to express her emotions creatively. Creating art helped her process her feelings and provided a positive outlet for her stress. Rachel also engaged in recreational activities, such as yoga and hiking, which improved her physical and mental well-being.

Rachel's family played a crucial role in her recovery journey. They attended family therapy sessions, where they learned about PTSD and how to support Rachel effectively. Her parents maintained open communication with Rachel, validating her feelings and providing a stable and supportive environment at home.

Over time, Rachel's symptoms began to improve. She became more confident in managing her anxiety and felt more connected to her family, friends, and school. Rachel's journey to recovery was marked by her resilience, determination, and the comprehensive support she received from her family, school, peers, and community resources.

Rachel's story highlights the importance of a multi-faceted support system for children and adolescents with PTSD. By accessing therapy, school support, peer groups, and community resources, young survivors can overcome their challenges and achieve significant improvements in their mental health and overall well-being.

A young survivor's journey involves seeking help, building a support network, and engaging in therapeutic activities. With the right support and determination, children and adolescents with PTSD can navigate their recovery and thrive.

CHAPTER 19: PTSD AND SUBSTANCE ABUSE

The relationship between PTSD and substance abuse is complex and multifaceted. Many individuals with PTSD turn to substances as a way to cope with their symptoms, leading to the development of co-occurring disorders. Understanding this link is essential for providing effective treatment and support.

The Link Between PTSD and Substance Abuse:

1. Self-Medication Hypothesis:
   - Individuals with PTSD often use substances such as alcohol, drugs, or prescription medications to self-medicate and alleviate their symptoms. This can temporarily reduce anxiety, numb emotional pain, or help with sleep difficulties.

2. Increased Vulnerability:
   - The emotional and psychological distress caused by PTSD can increase vulnerability to substance abuse. The need to escape from intrusive memories, flashbacks, and heightened arousal can lead individuals to seek relief through substances.

3. Reinforcement of Substance Use:
   - The temporary relief provided by substances can reinforce their use, creating a cycle of dependence. Over time, the individual may become reliant on substances to manage their PTSD symptoms, leading to addiction.

4. Impact of Substance Abuse on PTSD:
   - Substance abuse can exacerbate PTSD symptoms, leading to a worsening of the condition. It can also interfere with treatment and recovery efforts, making it more difficult for individuals to manage their PTSD.

5. Common Co-Occurring Disorders:
   - Individuals with PTSD are at higher risk for developing co-occurring disorders such as depression, anxiety disorders, and other mental health conditions. These co-occurring disorders can further complicate the relationship between PTSD and substance abuse.

After experiencing a traumatic event, Alex turned to alcohol as a way to cope with his PTSD symptoms. Initially, drinking helped him feel more relaxed and less anxious. However, over time, Alex became dependent on alcohol to manage his emotions. His PTSD symptoms worsened, and he found it increasingly difficult to function without drinking. Recognizing the impact of substance abuse on his PTSD was the first step toward seeking help and beginning his recovery journey.

Understanding the link between PTSD and substance abuse involves recognizing the factors that contribute to the use of substances as a coping mechanism and the impact of substance abuse on PTSD symptoms. Addressing both conditions is crucial for effective treatment and recovery.

Recognizing Substance Abuse as a Coping Mechanism

Identifying substance abuse as a coping mechanism for PTSD is a critical step in addressing both conditions. Recognizing the signs of substance abuse and understanding its role in managing PTSD symptoms can help individuals seek appropriate treatment.

Signs of Substance Abuse:

1. Behavioral Changes:
   - Increased Consumption: Noticeable increase in the use of alcohol or drugs, including prescription medications.
   - Changes in Habits: Altered daily routines, neglect of responsibilities, and changes in social behavior.
   - Risky Behaviors: Engaging in risky behaviors such as driving under the influence, unsafe sex, or illegal activities to obtain substances.

2. Physical Symptoms:
   - Withdrawal Symptoms: Experiencing withdrawal symptoms such as shaking, sweating, nausea, or anxiety when not using the substance.
   - Tolerance: Needing to use larger amounts of the substance to achieve the same effects.
   - Health Issues: Development of health problems related to substance use, such as liver damage, respiratory issues, or frequent infections.

3. Emotional and Psychological Changes:
   - Mood Swings: Frequent mood swings, irritability, or agitation.
   - Depression and Anxiety: Worsening of depression, anxiety, or other mental health conditions.
   - Isolation: Withdrawal from family, friends, and activities that were once enjoyed.

Understanding Substance Abuse as a Coping Mechanism:

1. Temporary Relief: Substances can provide temporary relief from PTSD symptoms, such as reducing anxiety, numbing emotional pain, or helping with sleep difficulties. This relief reinforces the use of substances as a coping mechanism.

2. Avoidance of Emotions: Substance abuse can serve as a way to avoid dealing with painful emotions and memories associated with trauma. By numbing these feelings, individuals may feel a

temporary escape from their distress.

3. Cycle of Dependence: The temporary relief provided by substances can lead to a cycle of dependence. As the effects of the substance wear off, PTSD symptoms may return, prompting further use to achieve relief.

4. Interference with Recovery: Substance abuse can interfere with the recovery process by hindering the effectiveness of therapy and other treatments for PTSD. It can also create additional physical and mental health challenges.

Addressing Substance Abuse as a Coping Mechanism:
1. Acknowledgment: Recognizing and acknowledging substance abuse as a coping mechanism is the first step toward seeking help. Understanding the reasons behind substance use can provide insight into the underlying issues.

2. Seeking Professional Help: Professional help is essential for addressing both PTSD and substance abuse. Therapists, counselors, and addiction specialists can provide comprehensive treatment plans that address both conditions.

3. Developing Healthy Coping Strategies: Learning and practicing healthy coping strategies, such as mindfulness, relaxation techniques, and exercise, can help individuals manage their PTSD symptoms without relying on substances.

4. Support Systems: Building a strong support system of family, friends, and support groups can provide encouragement and accountability during the recovery process.

After a traumatic incident, Sarah began using prescription painkillers to manage her PTSD symptoms. She found that the medication helped her feel more relaxed and less anxious. However, as her dependence on the medication grew, she began to experience withdrawal symptoms and health issues. Sarah's therapist helped her recognize that she was using the medication as a coping mechanism for her PTSD. With professional help, Sarah developed healthier coping strategies and began her journey to recovery from both PTSD and substance abuse.

Recognizing substance abuse as a coping mechanism for PTSD involves identifying the signs of substance use and understanding its role in managing symptoms. Addressing both conditions through professional help and healthy coping strategies is essential for effective recovery.

Effective Treatments for Co-Occurring Disorders

Treating co-occurring disorders of PTSD and substance abuse requires an integrated approach that addresses both conditions simultaneously. Effective treatments involve a combination of therapies, medications, and support systems designed to promote recovery and well-being.

Integrated Treatment Approaches:

1. Trauma-Informed Care:
   - Understanding Trauma: Treatment providers must understand the impact of trauma on individuals and how it relates to substance abuse. Trauma-informed care ensures that treatment is sensitive to the individual's experiences and needs.
   - Creating a Safe Environment: Providing a safe and supportive environment is essential for building trust and promoting recovery.

2. Cognitive Behavioral Therapy (CBT):
   - Addressing Negative Thought Patterns: CBT helps individuals identify and change negative thought patterns related to trauma and substance abuse.
   - Developing Coping Skills: CBT teaches healthy coping skills to manage PTSD symptoms and reduce reliance on substances.

3. Dialectical Behavior Therapy (DBT):
   - Emotional Regulation: DBT focuses on teaching skills for emotional regulation, distress tolerance, and interpersonal

effectiveness.
- Reducing Self-Destructive Behaviors: DBT is effective in reducing self-destructive behaviors, including substance abuse, by promoting healthier coping mechanisms.

4. Eye Movement Desensitization and Reprocessing (EMDR):
- Processing Trauma: EMDR helps individuals process traumatic memories and reduce the emotional distress associated with them.
- Reducing PTSD Symptoms: EMDR has been shown to be effective in reducing PTSD symptoms, which can decrease the need for substances as a coping mechanism.

5. Medication-Assisted Treatment (MAT):
- Managing Withdrawal and Cravings: MAT involves the use of medications to manage withdrawal symptoms and cravings associated with substance abuse.
- Supporting Mental Health: Medications such as antidepressants and anti-anxiety medications can help manage PTSD symptoms and support overall mental health.

Comprehensive Support Systems:

1. Support Groups:
- Peer Support: Support groups provide a sense of community and understanding. Groups such as Alcoholics Anonymous (AA) and Narcotics Anonymous (NA) offer support for individuals struggling with substance abuse.
- Trauma-Specific Groups: Groups specifically for individuals with co-occurring PTSD and substance abuse can provide targeted support and resources.

2. Family Involvement:
- Family Therapy: Involving family members in therapy can improve communication, support, and understanding. Family therapy addresses the impact of co-occurring disorders on the family dynamic.
- Education and Support: Educating family members about

PTSD and substance abuse can help them provide effective support and reduce stigma.

3. Holistic Approaches:
   - Mindfulness and Relaxation Techniques: Mindfulness practices, meditation, and relaxation techniques can help individuals manage stress and anxiety without relying on substances.
   - Physical Activity: Regular physical activity can improve mental health, reduce stress, and support overall well-being.
4. Case Management:
   - Coordinated Care: Case managers can help coordinate care, ensuring that individuals receive comprehensive services that address both PTSD and substance abuse.
   - Access to Resources: Case managers can connect individuals with resources such as housing, employment, and financial assistance.

After developing PTSD from a traumatic event, David began using drugs to cope with his symptoms. His addiction worsened his PTSD, and he struggled to find effective treatment. David entered a comprehensive treatment program that included trauma-informed care, CBT, and MAT. He also participated in support groups and family therapy. With an integrated approach that addressed both his PTSD and substance abuse, David made significant progress in his recovery. He developed healthier coping mechanisms and rebuilt his relationships with family and friends.

Effective treatments for co-occurring disorders of PTSD and substance abuse involve an integrated

approach that includes trauma-informed care, therapy, medication, and support systems. Addressing both conditions simultaneously is essential for promoting recovery and overall well-being.

Recovery from Dual Diagnoses

At the age of 30, Aaron experienced a traumatic event that left him struggling with severe PTSD. To cope with his symptoms, he turned to alcohol, which provided temporary relief but quickly led to dependence. Aaron's life began to spiral out of control as his alcohol use worsened his PTSD symptoms and affected his relationships, job, and overall well-being.

Recognizing the need for help, Aaron decided to seek treatment for both his PTSD and substance abuse. He entered a comprehensive treatment program that focused on addressing both conditions simultaneously. The program provided trauma-informed care, ensuring that Aaron's experiences and needs were understood and respected.

Aaron began trauma-focused cognitive behavioral therapy (TF-CBT) to address his PTSD symptoms. Through therapy, he learned to process his traumatic memories and develop healthier coping strategies. His therapist helped him understand the connection between his trauma and substance use, and together they worked on breaking the cycle of dependence.

In addition to therapy, Aaron participated in medication-assisted treatment (MAT) to manage his alcohol cravings and withdrawal symptoms. The medications helped stabilize his mood and reduce his reliance on alcohol as a coping mechanism.

Aaron also joined a support group for individuals with co-occurring PTSD and substance abuse. The group provided a sense of community and understanding, allowing him to share his experiences and receive support from others facing similar challenges. The camaraderie and encouragement he found in the group were instrumental in his recovery journey.

To further support his recovery, Aaron engaged in holistic practices such as mindfulness meditation and regular physical activity. These practices helped him manage stress, reduce anxiety, and improve his overall well-being. Aaron also involved his family in his recovery process, attending family therapy sessions that improved communication and strengthened their support system.

With the combination of therapy, medication, support groups, and holistic practices, Aaron made significant progress in his recovery. He developed healthier coping mechanisms, reduced his PTSD symptoms, and overcame his dependence on alcohol. Aaron's journey was marked by resilience, determination, and the support of a comprehensive treatment program.

Aaron's story is a testament to the possibility of recovery from dual diagnoses of PTSD and substance abuse. By seeking help, engaging in integrated treatment, and building a strong support system, individuals can overcome their challenges and achieve significant improvements in their mental health and overall well-being.

Recovery from dual diagnoses involves addressing both PTSD and substance abuse through comprehensive treatment and support. With the right resources and determination, individuals can break the cycle of dependence and lead fulfilling lives.

CHAPTER 20: LEGAL RIGHTS AND ADVOCACY

Understanding the legal rights of individuals with PTSD is essential for ensuring they receive appropriate support, protection, and accommodations. Legal rights span various areas, including employment, healthcare, and education, and knowing these rights can empower individuals to advocate for themselves effectively.

Understanding Legal Rights for Those with PTSD:

1. Americans with Disabilities Act (ADA):

- Protection Against Discrimination: The ADA prohibits discrimination against individuals with disabilities, including PTSD, in employment, public accommodations, and government services.

- Reasonable Accommodations: Employers are required to provide reasonable accommodations to employees with PTSD to enable them to perform their job duties. This can include flexible work hours, modified tasks, and access to mental health support.

2. Fair Housing Act (FHA):

- Equal Housing Opportunities: The FHA prohibits discrimination in housing based on disability. This ensures that individuals with PTSD have equal access to housing and can request reasonable accommodations from landlords.

3. Family and Medical Leave Act (FMLA):
   - Leave for Medical Reasons: The FMLA allows eligible employees to take unpaid leave for serious health conditions, including PTSD. This provides individuals with the time needed to seek treatment and manage their symptoms without fear of losing their job.

4. Health Insurance Portability and Accountability Act (HIPAA):
   - Privacy and Confidentiality: HIPAA protects the privacy of individuals' health information, ensuring that their PTSD diagnosis and treatment details are kept confidential. This law applies to healthcare providers, insurance companies, and employers.

5. Educational Rights:
   - Individualized Education Programs (IEP): Students with PTSD may be eligible for an IEP, which provides tailored support and accommodations to help them succeed in school. This can include modifications to assignments, additional time for tests, and access to counseling services.
   - Section 504 of the Rehabilitation Act: Section 504 ensures that students with disabilities, including PTSD, receive appropriate accommodations and support in educational settings.

6. Veterans' Rights:
   - VA Benefits: Veterans with PTSD may be eligible for various benefits through the Department of Veterans Affairs (VA), including disability compensation, healthcare, and vocational rehabilitation. The VA provides specialized programs and services to support veterans with PTSD.

Ensuring Legal Rights Are Upheld:

1. Documentation: Keep detailed records of PTSD diagnoses, treatment plans, and any related communications

with employers, landlords, or educational institutions. Documentation can support claims for accommodations and protect against discrimination.

2. Legal Assistance: Seek legal assistance from organizations that specialize in disability rights and advocacy. These organizations can provide guidance, representation, and support in navigating legal challenges.

3. Advocacy Groups: Engage with advocacy groups that focus on mental health and disability rights. These groups can provide resources, support, and a platform for raising awareness about PTSD-related issues.

After being diagnosed with PTSD, Maria struggled to maintain her job due to the symptoms she was experiencing. She was unaware of her rights under the ADA and hesitated to request accommodations. After connecting with a local disability rights organization, Maria learned about her legal rights and received support in advocating for reasonable accommodations at work. With the necessary accommodations in place, Maria was able to manage her symptoms more effectively and continue her employment.

Understanding legal rights is crucial for individuals with PTSD to ensure they receive appropriate support and protection. By being informed and seeking assistance, individuals can advocate for themselves and uphold their legal rights.

Navigating the Healthcare System

Navigating the healthcare system can be challenging for individuals with PTSD. Understanding the available resources, treatment options, and how to advocate for one's needs can improve access to effective care and support.

Accessing Healthcare Services:

1. Primary Care Providers:

- Initial Contact: Primary care providers (PCPs) are often the first point of contact for individuals seeking help for PTSD. PCPs can provide initial assessments, referrals to specialists, and ongoing care.

- Building Relationships: Establishing a trusting relationship with a PCP can facilitate ongoing support and coordination of care.

2. Mental Health Professionals:

- Specialized Care: Mental health professionals, including psychologists, psychiatrists, and licensed therapists, provide specialized care for PTSD. They offer various treatment modalities, such as therapy and medication management.

- Finding the Right Provider: Researching and finding a provider experienced in treating PTSD can significantly impact the effectiveness of treatment.

3. Community Mental Health Centers:

- Accessible Services: Community mental health centers offer accessible mental health services, often on a sliding fee scale. These centers provide therapy, medication management, and support groups.

Insurance and Coverage:

1. Understanding Insurance Plans:

- Coverage for Mental Health: Review insurance plans to understand coverage for mental health services, including therapy, medication, and hospital stays. The Mental Health Parity and Addiction Equity Act requires most insurance plans to provide equal coverage for mental health and physical health services.

- In-Network Providers: Identify in-network providers to reduce out-of-pocket costs. Insurance companies often provide directories of covered providers.

2. Medicaid and Medicare:

- Eligibility and Benefits: Medicaid and Medicare provide

coverage for mental health services for eligible individuals. Medicaid offers services for low-income individuals, while Medicare covers those over 65 and individuals with certain disabilities.

- Applying for Coverage: Understanding the application process and eligibility requirements can help individuals access these programs.

3. Veterans' Healthcare:

- VA Services: Veterans with PTSD can access specialized healthcare services through the VA. This includes therapy, medication management, and support programs tailored to veterans' needs.

- Enrolment: Veterans should enroll in the VA healthcare system to access these benefits. Information on eligibility and enrolment is available through the VA.

Advocating for Healthcare Needs:

1. Clear Communication:

- Expressing Needs: Clearly communicating symptoms, concerns, and treatment preferences to healthcare providers is essential. Preparing questions and discussing treatment options can improve care.

- Documentation: Keeping detailed records of symptoms, treatments, and communications with providers can help track progress and ensure comprehensive care.

2. Seeking Second Opinions:

- Exploring Options: If unsatisfied with a diagnosis or treatment plan, seeking a second opinion from another healthcare provider can provide additional perspectives and options.

- Empowerment: Seeking second opinions empowers individuals to make informed decisions about their healthcare.

3. Utilizing Patient Advocates:

- Support and Guidance: Patient advocates can assist in

navigating the healthcare system, addressing concerns, and ensuring that individuals receive appropriate care. Many hospitals and healthcare organizations offer patient advocacy services.

After being diagnosed with PTSD, John faced challenges in navigating the healthcare system and finding appropriate treatment. He struggled with understanding his insurance coverage and identifying experienced mental health providers. John sought assistance from a patient advocate who helped him understand his benefits, find an in-network therapist, and communicate effectively with his healthcare providers. With this support, John was able to access the care he needed and make progress in his recovery.

Navigating the healthcare system involves understanding available resources, insurance coverage, and advocating for one's needs. With the right support and knowledge, individuals with PTSD can access effective care and support.

Advocating for Oneself and Others

Advocacy plays a crucial role in ensuring that individuals with PTSD receive the support, accommodations, and treatment they need. Learning how to advocate for oneself and others can lead to significant improvements in mental health care and overall well-being.

Self-Advocacy:

1. Understanding One's Rights:
   - Legal Protections: Being aware of legal rights under laws such as the ADA, FMLA, and HIPAA empowers individuals to request necessary accommodations and protect their privacy.
   - Employment Rights: Knowing one's rights in the workplace can help secure reasonable accommodations and prevent discrimination.

2. Communicating Needs:

- Clear Communication: Clearly expressing symptoms, concerns, and treatment preferences to healthcare providers, employers, and educators is essential. Preparing questions and discussing options can improve care and support.

- Documentation: Keeping detailed records of symptoms, treatments, and communications with providers can help track progress and ensure comprehensive care.

3. Seeking Support:

- Utilizing Resources: Engaging with support groups, therapy, and patient advocacy services can provide guidance and encouragement. These resources offer a platform for sharing experiences and receiving support.

- Building a Support Network: Creating a network of trusted friends, family, and professionals who understand, and support one's needs can provide emotional and practical assistance.

Advocating for Others:

1. Providing Education:

- Raising Awareness: Educating others about PTSD and its impact can reduce stigma and promote understanding. Sharing information through presentations, workshops, and social media can reach a broader audience.

- Supporting Peers: Offering support and resources to peers with PTSD can create a sense of community and empowerment.

2. Engaging in Policy Advocacy:

- Advocacy Groups: Joining or supporting advocacy groups that focus on mental health and disability rights can amplify efforts to improve policies and services for individuals with PTSD.

- Legislative Advocacy: Engaging in legislative advocacy by contacting lawmakers, participating in campaigns, and supporting relevant legislation can lead to systemic changes that benefit individuals with PTSD.

3. Creating Inclusive Environments:

- Workplace Advocacy: Advocating for inclusive workplace policies and practices, such as mental health awareness training and accommodations, can improve the work environment for individuals with PTSD.

- Educational Advocacy: Supporting inclusive practices in educational settings, such as individualized education plans (IEPs) and mental health resources, can help students with PTSD succeed.

After overcoming significant challenges related to

PTSD, Rachel decided to become an advocate for others facing similar struggles. She joined a local mental health advocacy group and began sharing her story to raise awareness about PTSD. Rachel also engaged in legislative advocacy, supporting policies that improved access to mental health care. Through her efforts, Rachel empowered others to seek help and contributed to positive changes in her community.

Advocating for oneself and others involves understanding legal rights, communicating needs, seeking support, and engaging in policy and community advocacy. By taking an active role in advocacy, individuals with PTSD can improve their own lives and contribute to broader changes that benefit the community.

Resources and Organizations for Support

Numerous resources and organizations provide support, information, and advocacy for individuals with PTSD. These resources can offer valuable assistance in navigating the challenges associated with PTSD and accessing the necessary care and support.

National Organizations:

1. National Center for PTSD:
- Overview: The National Center for PTSD, part of the U.S. Department of Veterans Affairs, provides resources and research on PTSD.

- Services: The center offers educational materials, treatment options, and self-help tools for individuals with PTSD and their families.

2. Anxiety and Depression Association of America (ADAA):
   - Overview: ADAA focuses on improving the lives of individuals with anxiety, depression, and related disorders, including PTSD.
   - Services: The organization offers resources, educational materials, and a directory of mental health professionals.

3. Substance Abuse and Mental Health Services Administration (SAMHSA):
   - Overview: SAMHSA provides resources and support for individuals with mental health and substance use disorders.
   - Services: The organization offers a national helpline, treatment locators, and educational materials on PTSD and co-occurring disorders.

4. NAMI (National Alliance on Mental Illness):
   - Overview: NAMI is a grassroots organization dedicated to building better lives for individuals with mental illness, including PTSD.
   - Services: NAMI offers support groups, educational programs, and advocacy resources.

Veterans' Organizations:

1. Veterans Crisis Line:
   - Overview: The Veterans Crisis Line provides confidential crisis support for veterans and their families.
   - Services: The line offers 24/7 support through phone, text, and online chat.

2. Wounded Warrior Project:
   - Overview: The Wounded Warrior Project supports veterans and service members with PTSD and other injuries.
   - Services: The organization offers mental health programs,

peer support, and advocacy services.

3. Disabled American Veterans (DAV):
   - Overview: DAV provides support and advocacy for veterans with disabilities, including PTSD.
   - Services: The organization offers benefits assistance, advocacy, and support services.

Community Resources:

1. Local Mental Health Centers:
   - Overview: Community mental health centers provide accessible mental health services, often on a sliding fee scale.
   - Services: These centers offer therapy, medication management, and support groups.
2. Peer Support Groups:
   - Overview: Peer support groups offer a sense of community and understanding for individuals with PTSD.
   - Services: Groups such as Alcoholics Anonymous (AA), Narcotics Anonymous (NA), and PTSD-specific groups provide support and resources.

3. Educational Institutions:
   - Overview: Schools and universities often offer counseling services and support for students with PTSD.
   - Services: Educational institutions provide therapy, academic accommodations, and mental health resources.

Online Resources:

1. PTSD Coach:
   - Overview: PTSD Coach is a mobile app designed to help individuals manage PTSD symptoms.
   - Services: The app offers self-assessment tools, coping strategies, and educational materials.

2. Psychology Today:
   - Overview: Psychology Today offers a directory of mental health professionals and articles on various mental health

topics, including PTSD.

   - Services: The directory helps individuals find therapists and counselors experienced in treating PTSD.

3. Support Forums:

   - Overview: Online support forums provide a platform for individuals with PTSD to connect and share experiences.

   - Services: Forums such as PTSD Forum and MyPTSD offer peer support and resources.

After struggling to find the right support for her PTSD, Lisa discovered the National Center for PTSD and NAMI through an online search. She accessed their resources and connected with local support groups. These organizations provided valuable information and support, helping Lisa navigate her recovery journey.

Resources and organizations offer essential support for individuals with PTSD. By accessing these resources, individuals can find the help they need to manage their symptoms, seek treatment, and advocate for themselves and others.

Empowerment through Advocacy

At 25, Carlos was diagnosed with PTSD after experiencing a traumatic event during his deployment in the military. Struggling with flashbacks, anxiety, and depression, Carlos found it challenging to navigate daily life. He felt isolated and unsure of where to turn for help.

Determined to take control of his recovery, Carlos began researching his legal rights and available resources. He discovered the Americans with Disabilities Act (ADA) and learned that he was entitled to reasonable accommodations at work. Armed with this knowledge, Carlos approached his employer and requested accommodations, such as flexible work hours and a quiet space for breaks. His employer granted these accommodations, which significantly improved Carlos's ability to manage his symptoms at work.

Carlos also sought support from veterans' organizations, including the Wounded Warrior Project and Disabled American Veterans (DAV). These organizations provided valuable resources, including mental health programs, peer support, and advocacy services. Through these connections, Carlos found a sense of community and understanding, which was crucial for his recovery.

Inspired by his experiences, Carlos decided to become an advocate for other veterans with PTSD. He joined a local mental health advocacy group and began sharing his story to raise awareness about PTSD and the importance of support and accommodations. Carlos also participated in legislative advocacy, supporting policies that improved access to mental health care for veterans.

Through his advocacy efforts, Carlos empowered other veterans to seek help and advocate for their rights. He contributed to positive changes in his community and helped reduce the stigma associated with PTSD. Carlos's journey demonstrated the power of self-advocacy and the impact of collective efforts to improve mental health care.

Carlos's story highlights the importance of understanding legal rights, accessing resources, and engaging in advocacy. By taking an active role in his recovery and supporting others, Carlos found empowerment and contributed to broader changes that benefit the PTSD community.

Empowerment through advocacy involves understanding legal rights, seeking support, and actively participating in efforts to improve mental health care. By advocating for oneself and others, individuals with PTSD can create positive change and find strength in their journey.

CHAPTER 21: LONG-TERM MANAGEMENT

Long-term management of PTSD involves developing a comprehensive plan that addresses ongoing needs and promotes sustained well-being. A proactive approach to managing symptoms and maintaining mental health can help individuals lead fulfilling lives.

Developing a Long-Term Management Plan:

1. Personalized Approach:
   - Individual Needs: A long-term management plan should be tailored to the individual's specific needs, symptoms, and circumstances. This personalized approach ensures that the plan is effective and sustainable.
   - Assessment: Regular assessments with healthcare providers can help identify changes in symptoms and adjust the management plan accordingly.

2. Components of a Management Plan:
   - Therapy: Continued participation in therapy, such as Cognitive Behavioral Therapy (CBT) or Eye Movement Desensitization and Reprocessing (EMDR), can provide ongoing support and skill development.
   - Medication Management: For some individuals, medication may be a crucial component of their long-term plan. Regular consultations with a psychiatrist can ensure proper medication management.

- Self-Care Practices: Incorporating self-care practices, such as mindfulness, relaxation techniques, and physical activity, can support overall well-being and symptom management.

- Support Systems: Building and maintaining a strong support system of family, friends, and support groups is essential for long-term management.

3. Setting Goals:

- Short-Term Goals: Establishing short-term goals can provide a sense of accomplishment and motivate continued progress. These goals can be related to therapy, self-care, or personal achievements.

- Long-Term Goals: Long-term goals should focus on broader life aspirations, such as career development, relationships, and personal growth. These goals provide direction and purpose.

4. Monitoring Progress:

- Tracking Symptoms: Keeping a journal or using a symptom tracker can help individuals monitor their progress and identify patterns or triggers.

- Regular Check-Ins: Regular check-ins with healthcare providers ensure that the management plan remains effective, and adjustments are made as needed.

After years of struggling with PTSD, Jenna decided to develop a long-term management plan with the help of her therapist. Together, they identified her needs and set both short-term and long-term goals. Jenna continued therapy and incorporated self-care practices into her daily routine. She also joined a support group, which provided a sense of community and understanding. By monitoring her progress and adjusting her plan as needed, Jenna found stability and fulfillment in her life.

Developing a long-term management plan involves a personalized approach, setting goals, and monitoring progress. With a comprehensive plan in place, individuals with PTSD can manage their symptoms effectively and lead fulfilling lives.

The Importance of Routine and Structure

Establishing and maintaining a routine and structure is crucial for individuals with PTSD. A consistent routine can provide stability, reduce anxiety, and improve overall well-being.

Benefits of Routine and Structure:

1. Predictability and Control:
   - Reducing Uncertainty: A consistent routine reduces uncertainty and unpredictability, which can be sources of stress for individuals with PTSD.
   - Sense of Control: Routine provides a sense of control over one's environment and daily activities, contributing to a feeling of safety and stability.

2. Improved Mental Health:
   - Stress Reduction: Routine helps manage stress by providing a predictable schedule and reducing the need to make frequent decisions.
   - Better Sleep: Consistent sleep schedules improve sleep quality, which is often disrupted in individuals with PTSD.

3. Enhanced Productivity:
   - Structured Activities: A structured day promotes productivity and helps individuals accomplish tasks and goals.
   - Time Management: Routine improves time management skills, allowing individuals to balance work, self-care, and leisure activities.

4. Support for Coping Mechanisms:
   - Incorporating Self-Care: Routine can include self-care practices such as mindfulness, exercise, and relaxation techniques, which are essential for managing PTSD symptoms.
   - Scheduled Therapy Sessions: Regularly scheduled therapy sessions ensure that individuals receive consistent support and can work on their goals.

Creating a Routine:

1. Daily Schedule:
   - Morning Routine: Establishing a morning routine sets a positive tone for the day. This can include activities such as exercise, meditation, or a healthy breakfast.
   - Work or School Schedule: Incorporating structured time for work or school activities promotes productivity and a sense of purpose.
   - Evening Routine: An evening routine can help unwind and prepare for restful sleep. This may include relaxation techniques, reading, or a calming hobby.

2. Incorporating Self-Care:
   - Physical Activity: Regular exercise is beneficial for both physical and mental health. Scheduling time for physical activity can improve mood and reduce anxiety.
   - Relaxation Techniques: Including relaxation techniques such as deep breathing, meditation, or yoga in the routine can help manage stress.
   - Hobbies and Interests: Engaging in hobbies and interests provides a sense of enjoyment and fulfillment.

3. Flexibility:
   - Adapting to Changes: While routine is important, it is also essential to be flexible and adapt to changes when necessary. This helps build resilience and prevents rigidity.
   - Balancing Routine and Spontaneity: Finding a balance between routine and spontaneity ensures that life remains enjoyable and fulfilling.

After being diagnosed with PTSD, Tom found that his symptoms were exacerbated by a lack of structure in his daily life. With the help of his therapist, Tom created a daily routine that included a morning exercise routine, scheduled work hours, and an evening relaxation routine. By sticking to this routine, Tom noticed significant improvements in his mood, anxiety levels, and overall well-being. The predictability and structure provided a sense of control and stability, helping Tom manage his PTSD symptoms more effectively.

The importance of routine and structure lies in their ability to provide predictability, reduce stress, and support mental health. By creating and maintaining a consistent routine, individuals with PTSD can improve their overall well-being and manage their symptoms more effectively.

Continuing Therapy and Support

Ongoing therapy and support are essential components of long-term management for individuals with PTSD. Continued engagement in therapy and support systems can provide stability, help manage symptoms, and promote sustained recovery.

Benefits of Continuing Therapy:

1. Ongoing Skill Development:
   - Coping Strategies: Therapy provides ongoing opportunities to develop and refine coping strategies for managing PTSD symptoms.
   - Emotional Regulation: Continued therapy helps individuals improve their emotional regulation skills, reducing the impact of stress and anxiety.

2. Addressing New Challenges:
   - Life Changes: Life changes, such as new jobs, relationships, or health issues, can present new challenges. Ongoing therapy provides support in navigating these changes.
   - Symptom Fluctuations: PTSD symptoms can fluctuate over time. Regular therapy sessions help address any exacerbations of symptoms and adjust treatment plans accordingly.

3. Maintaining Progress:
   - Consistent Support: Regular therapy sessions provide consistent support and accountability, helping individuals

maintain their progress and avoid setbacks.

- Preventing Relapse: Continued therapy reduces the risk of relapse by addressing emerging issues and reinforcing healthy coping mechanisms.

Types of Ongoing Therapy:

1. Individual Therapy:
- Personalized Support: Individual therapy provides personalized support tailored to the individual's specific needs and goals.
- Therapeutic Techniques: Various therapeutic techniques, such as Cognitive Behavioral Therapy (CBT), Eye Movement Desensitization and Reprocessing (EMDR), and Dialectical Behavior Therapy (DBT), can be used to address PTSD symptoms.

2. Group Therapy:
- Peer Support: Group therapy offers a sense of community and peer support. Sharing experiences with others who understand can reduce feelings of isolation.
- Skill Building: Group therapy sessions often focus on building coping skills and strategies for managing PTSD symptoms.

3. Family Therapy:
- Improving Communication: Family therapy helps improve communication and understanding within the family unit. It provides a space for family members to express their concerns and learn how to support their loved one with PTSD.
- Addressing Family Dynamics: Therapy can address family dynamics that may impact the individual's recovery and help develop healthier relationships.

Support Systems:

1. Support Groups:
- Shared Experiences: Support groups provide a platform for

individuals with PTSD to share their experiences and receive support from others facing similar challenges.

- Resources and Information: Support groups often provide valuable resources and information on managing PTSD and accessing additional support.

2. Community Resources:

- Mental Health Centers: Community mental health centers offer a range of services, including therapy, support groups, and educational programs.

- Online Resources: Online resources, such as forums and mental health websites, provide access to support and information from the comfort of one's home.

3. Peer Support:

- Mentorship Programs: Peer mentorship programs pair individuals with experienced peers who provide guidance, support, and encouragement.

- Friendship and Community: Building friendships and community connections can provide additional support and reduce feelings of isolation.

After completing an initial course of therapy for PTSD, Emily realized that continued support was crucial for maintaining her progress. She decided to continue with individual therapy sessions and joined a weekly support group. These ongoing therapy sessions and support from her peers helped Emily navigate new challenges and maintain her emotional well-being. The consistent support and skill-building opportunities provided by therapy and support groups were instrumental in her long-term management plan.

Continuing therapy and support are vital for long-term management of PTSD. Ongoing engagement in therapy, support groups, and community resources provides stability, helps manage symptoms, and promotes sustained recovery.

Adapting to Changes Over Time

Adapting to changes over time is an essential aspect of long-term management for individuals with PTSD. Life events, evolving symptoms, and new challenges require flexibility and the ability to adjust coping strategies and support systems.
Adapting to Life Changes:

1. Major Life Events:
   - New Jobs or Careers: Transitioning to a new job or career can be stressful. It is important to identify potential stressors and develop coping strategies to manage anxiety and maintain mental health.
   - Changes in Relationships: Changes in personal relationships, such as marriage, divorce, or the birth of a child, can impact mental health. Therapy and support can help navigate these changes and maintain emotional well-being.

2. Health Changes:
   - Physical Health Issues: Managing physical health issues alongside PTSD can be challenging. Coordinating care between mental health and physical health providers ensures comprehensive support.
   - Aging: As individuals age, their needs and abilities may change. Adapting coping strategies and support systems to accommodate these changes is essential.

3. Environmental Changes:
   - Relocation: Moving to a new home or city can be a significant source of stress. Establishing a new support network and routine can help ease the transition.
   - Changes in Living Situation: Changes in living situations, such as moving in with family or transitioning to assisted living, require adjustments in coping strategies and support systems.

Evolving Symptoms:
1. Symptom Fluctuations:
   - Monitoring Symptoms: Regularly monitoring symptoms

helps identify fluctuations and adjust the management plan accordingly.

- Seeking Support: Reaching out for additional support during periods of increased symptoms can prevent setbacks and promote stability.

2. New Symptoms:

- Identifying Triggers: Identifying and addressing new triggers is important for managing emerging symptoms. Therapy can help develop strategies to cope with new challenges.

- Adjusting Treatment: Adjusting treatment plans, including therapy and medication, ensures that evolving symptoms are effectively managed.

Maintaining Flexibility:

1. Adjusting Coping Strategies:

- Evaluating Effectiveness: Regularly evaluating the effectiveness of coping strategies helps identify what is working and what needs adjustment.

- Trying New Techniques: Being open to trying new coping techniques, such as mindfulness, creative therapies, or physical activities, can provide additional support.

2. Updating Support Systems:

- Expanding Networks: Continuously expanding support networks, including joining new support groups or community organizations, provides ongoing support and resources.

- Maintaining Connections: Staying connected with existing support systems ensures consistent support and reduces feelings of isolation.

3. Setting New Goals:

- Reassessing Goals: Periodically reassessing short-term and long-term goals ensures they remain relevant and achievable.

- Celebrating Achievements: Celebrating achievements and milestones promotes motivation and a sense of accomplishment.

Over the years, Mark experienced several major life changes, including a career transition and the birth of his first child. These changes brought new challenges to managing his PTSD. With the help of his therapist, Mark adapted his coping strategies to accommodate his new responsibilities. He also expanded his support network by joining a parenting group and connecting with other new fathers. By remaining flexible and open to change, Mark successfully navigated these transitions and maintained his mental health.

Adapting to changes over time involves monitoring symptoms, adjusting coping strategies, and updating support systems. Flexibility and openness to change are essential for effective long-term management of PTSD.

Living a Fulfilling Life

After years of struggling with PTSD, David was determined to create a fulfilling life for himself. He knew that long-term management of his symptoms would require a comprehensive and proactive approach. With the support of his therapist, David developed a long-term management plan that included continued therapy, self-care practices, and a strong support system.

David's plan began with regular therapy sessions, where he worked on refining his coping strategies and addressing any new challenges that arose. His therapist helped him set short-term and long-term goals, providing a sense of direction and purpose. Through therapy, David learned the importance of routine and structure in managing his symptoms. He established a daily routine that included a morning exercise regimen, structured work hours, and an evening relaxation routine.

In addition to therapy, David incorporated various self-care practices into his routine. He found that mindfulness meditation helped him manage stress and stay grounded. Regular physical activity, such as running and yoga, improved his mood and overall well-being. David also made time for hobbies and interests that brought him joy, such as painting and playing the guitar.

Building and maintaining a strong support system was a crucial part of David's long-term management plan. He joined a local support group for individuals with PTSD, where he found a sense of community and understanding. The group provided a safe space for him to share his experiences and receive support from others facing similar challenges. David also involved his family in his recovery journey, attending family therapy sessions to improve communication and strengthen their support system.

Over time, David faced several major life changes, including a career transition and a move to a new city. These changes required him to adapt his management plan and coping strategies. With the support of his therapist and support group, David navigated these transitions successfully. He expanded his support network by connecting with new friends and community organizations in his new city.

David's journey was marked by resilience, determination, and the support of a comprehensive management plan. By staying proactive and flexible, he was able to manage his PTSD symptoms effectively and create a fulfilling life for himself. David's story is a testament to the possibility of living a fulfilling life despite the challenges of PTSD.

David's story highlights the importance of developing a long-term management plan, maintaining routine and structure, continuing therapy and support, and adapting to changes over time. With the right support and strategies, individuals with PTSD can lead fulfilling lives and achieve their goals.

CHAPTER 22: INSPIRATIONAL STORIES OF RECOVERY

Inspirational stories of recovery offer hope and encouragement to individuals navigating the challenges of PTSD. These brief stories from survivors highlight the resilience and determination that can lead to healing and a fulfilling life.

Compilation of Brief Stories from Survivors:

1. Samantha's Journey:
   - After a traumatic car accident, Samantha struggled with severe PTSD. She found solace in art therapy, which allowed her to express her emotions creatively. Through regular therapy sessions and the support of her family, Samantha gradually regained her confidence and found joy in her artwork. Today, she shares her story to inspire others and promotes the benefits of creative expression for healing.

2. Michael's Path to Recovery:
   - As a combat veteran, Michael experienced intense PTSD symptoms upon returning home. He joined a veteran support group where he connected with peers who understood his struggles. Michael also engaged in mindfulness meditation and physical fitness programs, which helped him manage his

symptoms. With time, Michael found a sense of purpose in helping other veterans through their recovery journeys.

3. Emma's Transformation:

- Emma's PTSD stemmed from childhood abuse, leading to years of emotional turmoil. With the help of a compassionate therapist, she worked through her traumatic memories using EMDR. Emma also found strength in writing, using journaling as a tool to process her emotions. Today, she is an advocate for mental health awareness and supports others in their healing journeys.

4. Jake's Renewal:

- After witnessing a violent incident, Jake developed PTSD that affected his daily life. He sought help from a trauma specialist and participated in Cognitive Behavioral Therapy (CBT). Jake also joined a local running group, finding that physical activity helped reduce his anxiety. His commitment to therapy and self-care led to significant improvements in his mental health, and he now mentors others facing similar challenges.

5. Sophia's Empowerment:

- Sophia experienced PTSD after surviving a natural disaster. She felt isolated and overwhelmed by her symptoms. Joining a community support group provided Sophia with a network of understanding individuals. She also practiced yoga and breathing exercises to manage her stress. Sophia's journey of recovery empowered her to become a volunteer, helping disaster survivors rebuild their lives.

These stories of recovery demonstrate that healing is possible with the right support and determination. Each individual's journey is unique, but common themes of resilience, support, and proactive self-care emerge as key components of recovery.

Lessons Learned from Different Journeys

The journeys of PTSD survivors offer valuable lessons that can inspire and guide others on their path to recovery. These lessons highlight the importance of seeking help, building support networks, and maintaining resilience.

Key Lessons Learned:

1. Seeking Help is Crucial:
   - Professional Support: Engaging with mental health professionals, such as therapists and counselors, is essential for effective treatment and symptom management.
   - Early Intervention: Seeking help early can prevent symptoms from worsening and provide tools for coping with trauma.

2. Building a Strong Support Network:
   - Family and Friends: Involving loved ones in the recovery process provides emotional support and understanding.
   - Peer Support: Connecting with others who have similar experiences through support groups can reduce feelings of isolation and provide valuable insights.

3. Incorporating Self-Care Practices:
   - Mindfulness and Relaxation: Practices such as mindfulness meditation, yoga, and deep breathing can help manage stress and promote emotional regulation.
   - Physical Activity: Regular exercise improves physical health, reduces anxiety, and enhances overall well-being.

4. Finding Healthy Coping Mechanisms:
   - Creative Outlets: Engaging in creative activities like art, writing, or music can provide an outlet for expressing emotions and processing trauma.
   - Hobbies and Interests: Pursuing hobbies and interests brings joy and fulfillment, helping to shift focus from trauma to positive experiences.

5. Maintaining Flexibility and Adaptability:
   - Adjusting Plans: Being open to adjusting coping strategies and treatment plans as needed ensures continued progress and

effectiveness.

- Embracing Change: Adapting to life changes and new challenges with resilience promotes long-term recovery.

6. Celebrating Small Victories:

- Acknowledging Progress: Celebrating small victories and milestones in recovery boosts motivation and self-esteem.

- Focusing on Strengths: Recognizing and building on personal strengths fosters a sense of empowerment and capability.

After several years of struggling with PTSD, Maria learned the importance of seeking help and building a support network. She engaged in therapy, joined a support group, and practiced mindfulness meditation. Maria also found joy in gardening, which became a therapeutic hobby. By incorporating these lessons into her life, Maria experienced significant improvements in her mental health and overall well-being.

Lessons learned from the journeys of PTSD survivors emphasize the importance of seeking help, building support networks, incorporating self-care practices, and maintaining flexibility. These lessons can guide others on their path to recovery and inspire hope for a fulfilling life.

Finding Hope in Others' Experiences

Finding hope in the experiences of others can provide comfort and motivation for individuals navigating their own recovery journeys. Inspirational stories of resilience and triumph over PTSD demonstrate that healing is possible and encourage individuals to keep moving forward.

Sources of Hope:

1. Shared Experiences:

- Relatability: Hearing stories from others who have faced similar challenges can create a sense of relatability and understanding.

- Validation: Knowing that others have experienced and overcome similar struggles validates one's own experiences and emotions.

2. Examples of Resilience:
- Overcoming Adversity: Stories of individuals who have overcome significant adversity highlight the power of resilience and determination.
- Strength in Vulnerability: Seeing others share their vulnerabilities and still find strength can inspire individuals to embrace their own vulnerabilities and seek help.

3. Positive Outcomes:
- Success Stories: Success stories demonstrate that recovery is possible and that individuals can lead fulfilling lives despite their challenges.
- Achieving Goals: Hearing about others achieving their goals and aspirations can motivate individuals to pursue their own dreams and ambitions.

4. Supportive Communities:
- Community Support: Being part of a supportive community, whether online or in-person, provides a network of encouragement and solidarity.
- Shared Wisdom: Communities offer a platform for sharing wisdom, coping strategies, and resources, enhancing collective knowledge and support.

5. Role Models:
- Inspiration: Role models who have navigated their own recovery journeys and achieved success can serve as powerful sources of inspiration.
- Guidance: Role models can offer guidance and mentorship, helping individuals navigate their own paths to recovery.

After joining an online support group for individuals with PTSD, James found hope in the stories shared by other members. He was inspired by their resilience and the positive changes they had made in their lives. The support group provided James with valuable coping strategies and a sense of community. Encouraged by the experiences of others, James continued his therapy and pursued his passion for writing. Over time, he found that his symptoms improved, and he began to share his own story to inspire others.

Finding hope in others' experiences involves connecting with supportive communities, learning from success stories, and drawing inspiration from role models. These sources of hope can provide comfort, motivation, and a sense of belonging for individuals on their recovery journeys.

Celebrating Milestones in Recovery

Celebrating milestones in recovery is an essential part of the healing process. Recognizing and honouring progress, no matter how small, fosters motivation, boosts self-esteem, and reinforces the commitment to recovery.

Importance of Celebrating Milestones:

1. Acknowledging Progress:
   - Positive Reinforcement: Celebrating milestones provides positive reinforcement, encouraging individuals to continue their efforts and maintain momentum.
   - Building Confidence: Recognizing achievements builds confidence and reinforces the belief that recovery is possible.

2. Motivating Continued Effort:
   - Setting Goals: Celebrating milestones helps set and achieve both short-term and long-term goals, providing a sense of direction and purpose.
   - Sustaining Motivation: Regularly celebrating progress sustains motivation and prevents burnout during the recovery journey.

3. Enhancing Emotional Well-Being:
   - Boosting Morale: Celebrating achievements boosts morale

and promotes a positive outlook, reducing feelings of hopelessness or frustration.

- Improving Self-Esteem: Recognizing personal accomplishments enhances self-esteem and self-worth, fostering a healthier self-image.

Ways to Celebrate Milestones:

1. Personal Celebrations:

- Journaling Achievements: Keeping a journal to document and reflect on achievements provides a tangible record of progress.

- Rewarding Yourself: Treating yourself to something special, such as a favorite meal or a relaxing activity, acknowledges your hard work and dedication.

2. Sharing with Others:

- Family and Friends: Sharing milestones with family and friends allows them to celebrate with you and provides additional support and encouragement.

- Support Groups: Celebrating milestones within a support group fosters a sense of community and collective pride in each other's progress.

3. Creating Rituals:

- Symbolic Actions: Creating rituals, such as lighting a candle or planting a tree, can symbolize progress and provide a meaningful way to mark milestones.

- Commemorative Items: Collecting commemorative items, such as charms or bracelets, can serve as physical reminders of achievements and progress.

4. Setting New Goals:

- Reflecting on Achievements: Reflecting on past achievements helps set new goals and provides a sense of direction for the next steps in recovery.

- Planning Future Milestones: Planning future milestones and visualizing their celebration motivates continued effort and commitment.

After a year of dedicated therapy and self-care, Lily decided to celebrate her progress by hosting a small gathering with her close friends and family. She shared her journey and the milestones she had achieved, from managing her symptoms to pursuing her passion for photography. The celebration not only honoured Lily's achievements but also strengthened her support network and inspired her to continue her recovery journey.

Celebrating milestones in recovery involves acknowledging progress, setting new goals, and sharing achievements with others. These celebrations foster motivation, boost self-esteem, and enhance overall well-being, reinforcing the commitment to a fulfilling and healthy life.

The Power of Resilience

At 28, Anna was diagnosed with PTSD following a traumatic event. The symptoms were overwhelming, and she felt like her life was unravelling. Determined to regain control, Anna sought help from a therapist specializing in trauma. Her journey to recovery was challenging, but Anna's resilience and determination helped her overcome numerous obstacles.

Anna's recovery journey began with Cognitive Behavioral Therapy (CBT), where she learned to identify and challenge negative thought patterns. She also practiced mindfulness meditation, which helped her stay present and manage her anxiety. Anna's therapist encouraged her to set both short-term and long-term goals, providing a sense of direction and purpose.

One of Anna's significant milestones was returning to work. She communicated with her employer about her condition and requested reasonable accommodations, such as flexible work hours and a quieter workspace. With these accommodations in place, Anna gradually regained her confidence and productivity at work.

Anna also found strength in physical activity. She joined a local yoga class, which not only improved her physical health but also provided a supportive community. The camaraderie and encouragement from her fellow yoga practitioners played a crucial role in her recovery.

Another critical aspect of Anna's journey was building a strong support network. She joined a support group for individuals with PTSD, where she connected with others who understood her struggles. Sharing experiences and coping strategies with her peers reduced her feelings of isolation and provided valuable insights into managing her symptoms.

Over time, Anna faced new challenges, such as a significant health issue and a move to a new city. These changes required her to adapt her coping strategies and support systems. With the help of her therapist and support network, Anna navigated these transitions successfully. She expanded her support network by connecting with new friends and community organizations in her new city.

Throughout her journey, Anna celebrated her milestones, no matter how small. She kept a journal to document her achievements and reflect on her progress. Celebrating these milestones provided positive reinforcement and motivated her to continue her efforts.

Anna's story is a testament to the power of resilience. Her determination to seek help, build a support network, and adapt to changes allowed her to manage her PTSD symptoms effectively and create a fulfilling life. Anna now shares her story to inspire others and advocate for mental health awareness.

The power of resilience lies in the ability to seek help, build support systems, and adapt to challenges. Anna's journey demonstrates that with determination and the right support, individuals with PTSD can overcome obstacles and lead fulfilling lives.

CHAPTER 23: CREATING A NEW NORMAL

Creating a new normal after experiencing trauma involves redefining what normalcy means and finding ways to live a fulfilling life despite the challenges of PTSD. This process is deeply personal and requires embracing change, finding joy, and building resilience.

Redefining Normalcy Post-Trauma:

1. Acceptance of Change:
   - Acknowledging the Impact: Accepting that trauma has changed aspects of one's life is the first step towards creating a new normal. This acknowledgment allows individuals to process their experiences and begin healing.
   - Letting Go of the Past: While it is important to remember the past, letting go of the desire to return to the way things were before the trauma can help individuals focus on building a new future.

2. Setting Realistic Expectations:
   - Adjusting Goals: Setting realistic goals that consider the impact of PTSD helps individuals create achievable milestones. These goals should be flexible and adaptable to changes in symptoms and circumstances.
   - Self-Compassion: Practicing self-compassion involves being

kind to oneself and understanding that recovery is a gradual process. It is important to celebrate small victories and be patient with setbacks.

3. Developing New Routines:
   - Creating Structure: Establishing new routines and habits provides a sense of stability and control. Routine activities such as exercise, hobbies, and relaxation practices can help manage symptoms and promote well-being.
   - Incorporating Self-Care: Prioritizing self-care activities, such as mindfulness, meditation, and physical activity, supports mental and physical health. Self-care routines should be an integral part of the new normal.

4. Finding Meaning and Purpose:
   - Exploring Interests: Engaging in activities that bring joy and fulfilment helps individuals find new meaning and purpose in life. This could involve pursuing hobbies, volunteering, or learning new skills.
   - Setting Personal Goals: Setting personal goals that align with one's values and interests provides direction and motivation. These goals should focus on personal growth and development.

After surviving a traumatic event, Sarah struggled to adjust to her new reality. She realized that her old life was no longer attainable and decided to redefine what normalcy meant for her. With the help of her therapist, Sarah set realistic goals and developed new routines that included daily exercise and mindfulness practices. She also pursued her passion for painting, which provided a sense of purpose and joy. Over time, Sarah found that her new normal, although different from her past, was filled with growth, resilience, and fulfilment.

Redefining normalcy post-trauma involves accepting change, setting realistic expectations, developing new routines, and finding meaning and purpose. This process allows individuals to create a fulfilling life despite the challenges of PTSD.

Embracing Change and New Opportunities

Embracing change and seeking new opportunities are essential components of creating a new normal after trauma. By welcoming change and exploring new possibilities, individuals can discover new paths to fulfillment and growth.

Embracing Change:

1. Adapting to New Realities:
   - Flexibility: Being open to change and adapting to new circumstances is crucial for recovery. Flexibility allows individuals to adjust their plans and strategies as needed.
   - Resilience: Building resilience involves developing the ability to bounce back from setbacks and continue moving forward. This resilience is strengthened through experiences and coping strategies.

2. Positive Outlook:
   - Focusing on Strengths: Identifying and leveraging personal strengths can help individuals navigate change more effectively. Focusing on strengths builds confidence and a positive outlook.
   - Reframing Challenges: Viewing challenges as opportunities for growth and learning can shift the perspective from a negative to a positive mindset. This reframing encourages proactive problem-solving.

3. Support Systems:
   - Building Relationships: Maintaining strong relationships with family, friends, and support groups provides a network of encouragement and assistance. These connections offer emotional support and practical help during times of change.
   - Seeking Professional Help: Professional support from therapists and counselors can provide guidance and strategies for managing change. Ongoing therapy ensures that individuals have the tools needed to cope with new challenges.

Exploring New Opportunities:

1. Personal Growth:
   - Learning New Skills: Taking up new hobbies or learning new skills can provide a sense of accomplishment and joy. These activities can also open up new opportunities for personal and professional growth.
   - Setting New Goals: Setting new goals that align with one's interests and values provides direction and motivation. These goals should focus on growth, development, and exploring new possibilities.

2. Career Opportunities:
   - Career Change: Exploring new career opportunities or pursuing further education can lead to professional growth and fulfillment. A career change may provide a fresh start and new challenges.
   - Entrepreneurship: Starting a business or engaging in freelance work allows individuals to pursue their passions and create new opportunities for themselves.

3. Community Involvement:
   - Volunteering: Volunteering in the community can provide a sense of purpose and connection. It also allows individuals to contribute to causes they care about and make a positive impact.
   - Advocacy: Becoming an advocate for mental health awareness and support can be a powerful way to create change and support others. Advocacy work can provide a sense of purpose and fulfillment.

After experiencing trauma, John decided to embrace change and seek new opportunities. He left his previous job and pursued further education in a field he was passionate about. John also started volunteering at a local animal shelter, which provided a sense of purpose and joy. Through these new opportunities, John discovered new strengths and passions that enriched his life. Embracing change and seeking new opportunities allowed John to create a new normal that was fulfilling and meaningful.

Embracing change and exploring new opportunities are key to creating a new normal after trauma. By being open to change and seeking new paths, individuals can discover new sources of fulfillment and growth.

Building a Life of Joy and Fulfillment

Building a life of joy and fulfillment involves finding activities and practices that bring happiness, purpose, and meaning. It requires a proactive approach to seeking out positive experiences and creating a balanced and fulfilling life.

Key Elements of a Joyful and Fulfilling Life:

1. Pursuing Passions:
   - Identifying Interests: Discovering and pursuing interests and passions brings joy and a sense of purpose. This could involve hobbies, creative pursuits, or professional endeavors.
   - Engagement: Engaging in activities that are enjoyable and fulfilling provides a sense of accomplishment and satisfaction.

2. Nurturing Relationships:
   - Building Connections: Maintaining strong relationships with family, friends, and community members fosters a sense of belonging and support.
   - Quality Time: Spending quality time with loved ones and participating in social activities strengthens bonds and enhances emotional well-being.

3. Self-Care Practices:
   - Physical Health: Prioritizing physical health through regular exercise, a balanced diet, and adequate sleep supports overall well-being.
   - Mental Health: Engaging in self-care practices such as mindfulness, relaxation techniques, and therapy promotes mental health and reduces stress.

4. Personal Growth:

- Continuous Learning: Pursuing continuous learning and personal development opportunities fosters growth and keeps life interesting.
- Setting Goals: Setting and achieving personal goals provides direction and a sense of accomplishment.

5. Giving Back:
- Volunteering: Volunteering and helping others brings a sense of purpose and fulfillment. It allows individuals to make a positive impact in their community.
- Advocacy: Engaging in advocacy work for causes one is passionate about can be deeply fulfilling and create meaningful change.

6. Finding Balance:
- Work-Life Balance: Maintaining a healthy work-life balance ensures that individuals have time for both professional responsibilities and personal interests.
- Leisure and Relaxation: Incorporating leisure activities and relaxation into daily routines helps reduce stress and promote well-being.

After recovering from trauma, Emily focused on building a life filled with joy and fulfillment. She pursued her passion for photography, which brought her immense joy and satisfaction. Emily also nurtured her relationships with family and friends by spending quality time with them. She prioritized her physical and mental health through regular exercise and mindfulness practices. Emily found fulfillment in volunteering at a local shelter, where she made a positive impact in her community. By finding balance and pursuing her passions, Emily created a life that was joyful and fulfilling.

Building a life of joy and fulfillment involves pursuing passions, nurturing relationships, practicing self-care, seeking personal growth, giving back, and finding balance. These elements contribute to a well-rounded and meaningful life.

Thriving After Trauma

Jessica's journey to thriving after trauma began with a commitment to redefine her life and seek new opportunities for growth and fulfillment. After experiencing a traumatic event, Jessica struggled with severe PTSD symptoms that impacted her daily life. Determined to regain control and create a new normal, she sought the help of a trauma therapist who specialized in Cognitive Behavioral Therapy (CBT).

Through therapy, Jessica learned to identify and challenge negative thought patterns. She also practiced mindfulness meditation to stay present and manage her anxiety. With her therapist's support, Jessica set both short-term and long-term goals that provided a sense of direction and purpose.

One of Jessica's significant milestones was returning to work. She communicated with her employer about her condition and requested reasonable accommodations, such as flexible work hours and a quieter workspace. With these accommodations in place, Jessica gradually regained her confidence and productivity at work.

Jessica also embraced new opportunities for personal growth. She took up painting, a hobby she had always enjoyed but had set aside. Painting became a therapeutic outlet for her emotions and a source of joy. She also joined a local art club, where she met new friends and found a supportive community.

To further enhance her well-being, Jessica prioritized her physical health. She started a regular exercise routine that included yoga and jogging. The physical activity helped reduce her anxiety and improve her overall mood. Jessica also focused on maintaining a balanced diet and getting adequate sleep, which contributed to her overall health and energy levels.

In addition to her personal pursuits, Jessica found fulfillment in giving back to her community. She began volunteering at a local animal shelter, where she helped care for abandoned and rescued animals. Volunteering provided Jessica with a sense of purpose and connection, and she found joy in making a positive impact.

Throughout her journey, Jessica celebrated her milestones and achievements. She kept a journal to document her progress and reflect on her growth. Celebrating these milestones provided positive reinforcement and motivated her to continue her efforts.

Jessica's story is a testament to the possibility of thriving after trauma. Her determination to seek help, embrace new opportunities, and prioritize her well-being allowed her to overcome the challenges of PTSD and create a fulfilling life. Jessica now shares her story to inspire others and advocate for mental health awareness.

Thriving after trauma involves seeking help, embracing new opportunities, prioritizing well-being, and finding fulfillment in personal pursuits and giving back. Jessica's journey demonstrates that with resilience and support, individuals can overcome obstacles and lead joyful and meaningful lives.

Final Thoughts on Turning Adversity into Opportunity

Turning adversity into opportunity involves a mindset shift and a proactive approach to finding meaning and growth in challenging experiences. By embracing resilience, seeking support, and exploring new possibilities, individuals can transform their lives and create a new normal filled with joy and fulfillment.

Key Takeaways:

1. Resilience is Key:
   - Building Resilience: Developing resilience involves strengthening one's ability to cope with and recover from adversity. This can be achieved through therapy, self-care

practices, and building a strong support network.

- Embracing Challenges: Viewing challenges as opportunities for growth and learning helps build resilience and fosters a positive outlook.

2. Support Systems are Essential:

- Seeking Help: Professional support from therapists, counselors, and support groups is crucial for effective recovery and symptom management.

- Building Connections: Strong relationships with family, friends, and community members provide emotional support and practical assistance.

3. Personal Growth and Fulfillment:

- Pursuing Passions: Engaging in activities that bring joy and fulfillment helps individuals find new meaning and purpose in life.

- Continuous Learning: Pursuing continuous learning and personal development fosters growth and keeps life interesting.

4. Celebrating Milestones:

- Acknowledging Progress: Celebrating milestones and achievements provides positive reinforcement and motivation.

- Setting New Goals: Continuously setting and achieving new goals ensures ongoing growth and development.

5. Creating a New Normal:

- Redefining Normalcy: Redefining what normalcy means and creating new routines and habits provides stability and control.

- Embracing Change: Being open to change and exploring new opportunities allows individuals to discover new paths to fulfillment.

Final Thoughts:

Turning adversity into opportunity is a journey that requires resilience, support, and a proactive approach to finding joy and fulfillment. By embracing change, seeking help, and pursuing personal growth, individuals can transform their lives and create a new normal that is meaningful and fulfilling.

After experiencing a traumatic event, Michael struggled to find his way. Determined to turn his adversity into an opportunity for growth, he sought help from a therapist and joined a support group. Michael embraced new opportunities for personal and professional growth, including pursuing further education and volunteering in his community. Through his resilience and determination, Michael transformed his life and found new meaning and fulfillment. His journey is a testament to the power of turning adversity into opportunity.

The journey to turning adversity into opportunity involves embracing resilience, seeking support, and pursuing personal growth. With the right mindset and approach, individuals can overcome challenges and create a fulfilling and meaningful life.

CHAPTER 24: RESOURCES AND REFERENCES

Having access to a comprehensive list of resources is crucial for individuals navigating PTSD. This chapter provides a detailed list of books, articles, and studies on PTSD that can offer valuable insights, guidance, and support.

Comprehensive List of Books on PTSD:

1. "The Body Keeps the Score: Brain, Mind, and Body in the Healing of Trauma" by Bessel van der Kolk
   - Overview: This book explores how trauma impacts the brain and body, and offers insights into various therapeutic approaches for healing.

2. "Waking the Tiger: Healing Trauma" by Peter A. Levine
   - Overview: Peter Levine introduces the concept of Somatic Experiencing and provides practical tools for healing trauma through body awareness.

3. "In an Unspoken Voice: How the Body Releases Trauma and Restores Goodness" by Peter A. Levine
   - Overview: This book delves into the physiological aspects of trauma and offers techniques for recovery.

4. "Trauma and Recovery: The Aftermath of Violence—from Domestic Abuse to Political Terror" by Judith Herman

- Overview: Judith Herman examines the impact of trauma on individuals and society, and outlines stages of recovery.

5. "Healing from Trauma: A Survivor's Guide to Understanding Your Symptoms and Reclaiming Your Life" by Jasmin Lee Cori
- Overview: This guide offers practical advice and exercises for trauma survivors to understand their symptoms and begin the healing process.

Notable Articles and Studies on PTSD:

1. "Posttraumatic Stress Disorder: From Diagnosis to Prevention" (JAMA)
- Overview: This article provides an overview of PTSD, including diagnostic criteria, risk factors, and prevention strategies.

2. "The Effectiveness of EMDR Therapy for Treating PTSD" (Journal of EMDR Practice and Research)
- Overview: This study evaluates the effectiveness of Eye Movement Desensitization and Reprocessing (EMDR) therapy in treating PTSD.

3. "PTSD and Physical Health" (National Center for PTSD)
- Overview: This article explores the connection between PTSD and various physical health issues, including cardiovascular disease and chronic pain.

4. "The Role of Cognitive Behavioral Therapy in the Treatment of PTSD" (Cognitive and Behavioral Practice)
- Overview: This study examines the impact of Cognitive Behavioral Therapy (CBT) on PTSD symptoms and overall recovery.

5. "Mindfulness-Based Stress Reduction for Posttraumatic Stress Disorder" (Journal of Clinical Psychology)
- Overview: This research assesses the effectiveness of Mindfulness-Based Stress Reduction (MBSR) in reducing PTSD symptoms.

Research and Studies on PTSD:

1. "The Neurobiology of PTSD" (Harvard Review of Psychiatry)
   - Overview: This study explores the neurobiological mechanisms underlying PTSD and discusses potential implications for treatment.

2. "PTSD in Military Veterans: A Review of Prevalence and Risk Factors" (Military Medicine)
   - Overview: This review examines the prevalence of PTSD among military veterans and identifies key risk factors associated with the disorder.

3. "Trauma-Informed Care in Behavioral Health Services" (Substance Abuse and Mental Health Services Administration)
   - Overview: This report provides guidelines for implementing trauma-informed care practices in behavioral health services.

4. "The Impact of Childhood Trauma on Adult Mental Health" (Journal of Affective Disorders)
   - Overview: This study investigates the long-term effects of childhood trauma on adult mental health, including the development of PTSD.

5. "Group Therapy for PTSD: A Meta-Analysis" (Psychological Bulletin)
   - Overview: This meta-analysis evaluates the effectiveness of various group therapy approaches in treating PTSD.

Having access to these comprehensive resources can provide valuable insights and guidance for individuals with PTSD, their families, and professionals working in the field.

Organizations and Support Groups

Support from organizations and support groups is essential for individuals with PTSD. These resources offer a range of services, including counseling, peer support, and educational materials.

National Organizations:

1. National Center for PTSD:
   - Overview: Provides research, education, and support for individuals with PTSD.
   - Website: [National Center for PTSD](https://www.ptsd.va.gov/)

2. Anxiety and Depression Association of America (ADAA):
   - Overview: Offers resources and support for individuals with anxiety, depression, and PTSD.
   - Website: [ADAA](https://adaa.org/)

3. Substance Abuse and Mental Health Services Administration (SAMHSA):
   - Overview: Provides resources for mental health and substance use disorders.
   - Website: [SAMHSA](https://www.samhsa.gov/)

4. NAMI (National Alliance on Mental Illness):
   - Overview: Offers support, education, and advocacy for individuals with mental illness, including PTSD.
   - Website: [NAMI](https://www.nami.org/)

Veterans' Organizations:

1. Veterans Crisis Line:
   - Overview: Provides confidential crisis support for veterans and their families.
   - Website: [Veterans Crisis Line](https://www.veteranscrisisline.net/)

2. Wounded Warrior Project:
   - Overview: Supports veterans and service members with PTSD and other injuries.
   - Website: [Wounded Warrior Project](https://www.woundedwarriorproject.org/)

3. Disabled American Veterans (DAV):

- Overview: Provides support and advocacy for veterans with disabilities, including PTSD.
  - Website: [DAV](https://www.dav.org/)

Support Groups:

1. PTSD Alliance:
  - Overview: Offers support and resources for individuals with PTSD and their families.
  - Website: [PTSD Alliance](http://www.ptsdalliance.org/)

2. Sidran Institute:
  - Overview: Provides educational materials and support for trauma survivors.
  - Website: [Sidran Institute](https://www.sidran.org/)

3. Give an Hour:
  - Overview: Provides free mental health services to veterans and their families.
  - Website: [Give an Hour](https://giveanhour.org/)

4. Courage to Caregivers:
  - Overview: Offers support groups and resources for caregivers of individuals with PTSD.
  - Website: [Courage to Caregivers](https://www.couragetocaregivers.org/)

Local and Community Resources:

1. Community Mental Health Centers:
  - Overview: Local centers offering therapy, support groups, and educational programs.
  - Contact: Local health department or directory for contact information.

2. Peer Support Groups:
  - Overview: Groups like Alcoholics Anonymous (AA), Narcotics Anonymous (NA), and PTSD-specific groups provide peer support and resources.

- Contact: Local community centers or online directories for group information.

3. Educational Institutions:
   - Overview: Schools and universities offering counseling services and support for students with PTSD.
   - Contact: School counseling services or student health centers for more information.

Organizations and support groups provide essential services and resources for individuals with PTSD and their families. Engaging with these organizations can offer valuable support and a sense of community.

Online Resources and Forums

Online resources and forums offer accessible support, information, and community for individuals with PTSD. These platforms provide a space for sharing experiences, accessing educational materials, and connecting with others.

Online Resources:

1. PTSD Coach Online:
   - Overview: Provides self-help tools and resources for managing PTSD symptoms.
   - Website: [PTSD Coach Online](https://www.ptsd.va.gov/appvid/mobile/ptsdcoach_app.asp)

2. Mindful:
   - Overview: Offers articles, guides, and resources on mindfulness and meditation practices.
   - Website: [Mindful](https://www.mindful.org/)

3. Psychology Today:
   - Overview: Provides a directory of mental health professionals and articles on mental health topics, including PTSD.
   - Website: [Psychology Today](https://

www.psychologytoday.com/)

4. Headspace:
   - Overview: Offers guided meditation and mindfulness exercises to help manage stress and anxiety.
   - Website: [Headspace](https://www.headspace.com/)

5. Calm:
   - Overview: Provides guided meditations, sleep stories, and relaxation techniques.
   - Website: [Calm](https://www.calm.com/)

Online Forums:

1. MyPTSD:
   - Overview: An online community for individuals with PTSD to share experiences and receive support.
   - Website: [MyPTSD](https://www.myptsd.com/)

2. PTSD Forum:
   - Overview: An online forum for discussions on PTSD, treatment options, and support.
   - Website: [PTSD Forum](https://www.myptsd.com/c/forums/)

3. Reddit PTSD Community:
   - Overview: A subreddit for individuals with PTSD to share experiences, ask questions, and receive support.
   - Website: [Reddit PTSD](https://www.reddit.com/r/ptsd/)

4. Daily Strength PTSD Support Group:
   - Overview: An online support group offering discussions, advice, and encouragement for individuals with PTSD.
   - Website: [Daily Strength PTSD](https://www.dailystrength.org/group/post-traumatic-stress-disorder-ptsd)

Educational Websites:

1. National Institute of Mental Health (NIMH):

- Overview: Provides information on mental health disorders, including PTSD, research, and treatment options

.

- Website: [NIMH](https://www.nimh.nih.gov/)

2. Mayo Clinic:
- Overview: Offers comprehensive information on PTSD symptoms, causes, and treatment options.
- Website: [Mayo Clinic](https://www.mayoclinic.org/)

3. WebMD:
- Overview: Provides articles and resources on PTSD, including symptoms, diagnosis, and treatment.
- Website: [WebMD](https://www.webmd.com/)

4. HelpGuide:
- Overview: Offers practical information and resources for managing PTSD and other mental health conditions.
- Website: [HelpGuide](https://www.helpguide.org/)

Online resources and forums offer valuable support and information for individuals with PTSD. These platforms provide accessible ways to connect with others, learn about PTSD, and find helpful tools for managing symptoms.

Self-Help Tools and Apps

Self-help tools and apps can provide convenient and effective ways to manage PTSD symptoms, practice mindfulness, and improve overall mental health. These tools offer guided exercises, tracking features, and resources to support recovery.

Self-Help Tools:

1. Mindfulness Meditation:
- Guided Meditation: Various apps and online platforms offer guided meditation sessions to help manage stress and anxiety.
- Breathing Exercises: Techniques such as deep breathing and progressive muscle relaxation can help reduce tension and

promote relaxation.

2. Journaling:

- Expressive Writing: Keeping a journal to document thoughts, feelings, and experiences can provide a therapeutic outlet for processing emotions.

- Gratitude Journal: Focusing on positive experiences and things one is grateful for can enhance mood and well-being.

3. Relaxation Techniques:

- Visualization: Guided imagery and visualization exercises can help create a sense of calm and reduce anxiety.

- Grounding Techniques: Practicing grounding exercises can help individuals stay present and manage flashbacks or intrusive thoughts.

Helpful Apps:

1. PTSD Coach:

- Overview: Designed to help individuals with PTSD manage symptoms and find resources. The app offers self-assessment tools, coping strategies, and educational materials.

- Available on: [iOS](https://apps.apple.com/us/app/ptsd-coach/id430646302) | [Android](https://play.google.com/store/apps/details?id=gov.va.ptsd.ptsdcoach2)

2. Calm:

- Overview: Provides guided meditations, sleep stories, and relaxation techniques to help manage stress and anxiety.

- Available on: [iOS](https://apps.apple.com/us/app/calm/id571800810) | [Android](https://play.google.com/store/apps/details?id=com.calm.android)

3. Headspace:

- Overview: Offers guided meditation and mindfulness exercises designed to improve mental health and well-being.

- Available on: [iOS](https://apps.apple.com/us/app/headspace-meditation-sleep/id493145008) | [Android](https://

play.google.com/store/apps/details?
id=com.getsomeheadspace.android)

4. Insight Timer:
   - Overview: Features guided meditations, music tracks, and talks from mindfulness experts to support mental health.
   - Available on: [iOS](https://apps.apple.com/us/app/insight-timer-meditation-app/id337472899) | [Android](https://play.google.com/store/apps/details?id=com.spotlightsix.zentimerlite2)

5. Breathe2Relax:
   - Overview: Offers guided breathing exercises to help reduce stress and manage anxiety.
   - Available on: [iOS](https://apps.apple.com/us/app/breathe2relax/id425720246) | [Android](https://play.google.com/store/apps/details?id=org.t2health.breathe2relax)

Additional Tools:

1. Mood Tracking Apps:
   - Daylio: Allows users to track their mood, activities, and mental health trends.
   - Available on: [iOS](https://apps.apple.com/us/app/daylio-journal/id1194023242) | [Android](https://play.google.com/store/apps/details?id=net.daylio)

2. Sleep Apps:
   - Sleep Cycle: Tracks sleep patterns and provides insights to improve sleep quality.
   - Available on: [iOS](https://apps.apple.com/us/app/sleep-cycle-sleep-tracker/id320606217) | [Android](https://play.google.com/store/apps/details?id=com.northcube.sleepcycle)

3. Fitness Apps:
   - Nike Training Club: Offers a variety of workout routines and

fitness programs to improve physical health and reduce stress.
   - Available on: [iOS](https://apps.apple.com/us/app/nike-training-club/id301521403) | [Android](https://play.google.com/store/apps/details?id=com.nike.ntc)

Self-help tools and apps provide convenient and effective ways to manage PTSD symptoms and improve overall well-being. These resources offer guided exercises, tracking features, and educational materials to support recovery.

Encouragement to Continue the Journey

Recovery from PTSD is a journey that requires resilience, support, and a proactive approach to finding joy and fulfillment. The resources, tools, and stories provided in this book are meant to guide and support individuals on their path to healing.

Key Messages of Encouragement:

1. Resilience is Your Strength:
   - Building Resilience: Embrace your resilience as a powerful tool in your recovery. Every step forward, no matter how small, is a testament to your strength and determination.
   - Overcoming Setbacks: Understand that setbacks are a natural part of the recovery process. Use them as opportunities to learn, grow, and refine your strategies.

2. Support is Essential:
   - Seeking Help: Never hesitate to seek help from professionals, support groups, and loved ones. Support is crucial for navigating the challenges of PTSD and finding stability.
   - Building Connections: Foster strong relationships and build a support network that provides encouragement, understanding, and practical assistance.

3. Embrace Change and New Opportunities:
   - Adapting to New Normals: Embrace the changes that come with recovery and be open to new opportunities for growth and fulfillment.

- Exploring Passions: Pursue activities and interests that bring you joy and satisfaction. Discovering new passions can provide a sense of purpose and direction.

4. Celebrate Your Progress:
   - Acknowledging Achievements: Celebrate your milestones and achievements, no matter how small. Recognize the progress you have made and use it as motivation to continue moving forward.
   - Setting New Goals: Continuously set and work towards new goals that align with your values and aspirations. This keeps your recovery journey dynamic and fulfilling.

5. You Are Not Alone:
   - Shared Experiences: Remember that you are not alone in your journey. Many others have faced similar challenges and found ways to thrive. Their stories and experiences can offer hope and guidance.
   - Community Support: Engage with supportive communities, both online and in-person, to find solidarity and shared wisdom.

After years of struggling with PTSD, Alex found hope and encouragement through the stories and support of others. By seeking help, embracing change, and celebrating his progress, Alex transformed his life and created a new normal filled with joy and fulfillment. His journey is a reminder that recovery is possible and that with resilience and support, individuals can overcome adversity and find happiness.

Final Encouragement:

Your journey to recovery is unique and filled with opportunities for growth and fulfillment. Embrace your resilience, seek support, and remain open to new possibilities. Celebrate your progress and continue to pursue a life of joy and meaning. Remember, you have the strength and courage to turn adversity into opportunity and create a new normal that is vibrant and fulfilling.

CHAPTER 25: CONCLUSION

As we come to the end of this book, it is important to summarize the key points covered and reflect on the journey of healing. This book has aimed to provide comprehensive guidance and support for individuals dealing with PTSD, helping them turn adversity into opportunity.

Summary of Key Points Covered:

1. Understanding PTSD:
   - Definition and Symptoms: PTSD is a mental health condition triggered by experiencing or witnessing a traumatic event. Symptoms include flashbacks, nightmares, severe anxiety, and uncontrollable thoughts about the event.
   - Causes and Risk Factors: PTSD can result from various types of trauma, including combat exposure, natural disasters, accidents, and personal assaults.

2. The Journey to Diagnosis:
   - Recognizing Signs: Identifying the signs of PTSD in oneself and others is crucial for early intervention.
   - Seeking Professional Help: Consulting healthcare professionals for accurate diagnosis and effective treatment is essential.

3. Therapy and Treatment:
   - Types of Therapy: Various therapies, including Cognitive Behavioral Therapy (CBT), Eye Movement Desensitization and

Reprocessing (EMDR), and group therapy, have proven effective in treating PTSD.

- Medication: Medication can play a vital role in managing symptoms and supporting overall mental health.

4. Self-Help Strategies:

- Mindfulness and Meditation: Practicing mindfulness and meditation helps manage stress and improve emotional regulation.

- Exercise and Nutrition: Physical health, including regular exercise and a balanced diet, significantly impacts mental health.

5. Building a Support Network:

- Importance of Support: A strong support network of family, friends, and support groups provides essential emotional and practical assistance.

- Community and Online Resources: Engaging with community organizations and online forums offers additional support and resources.

6. Long-Term Management:

- Routine and Structure: Establishing a consistent routine and structure provides stability and control.

- Adapting to Changes: Flexibility and adaptability are key to managing evolving symptoms and life changes.

7. Inspirational Stories:

- Shared Experiences: Hearing from others who have successfully managed PTSD provides hope and encouragement.

- Personal Stories: Personal stories of resilience and recovery highlight the possibility of living a fulfilling life despite PTSD.

8. Resources and References:

- Books and Articles: A comprehensive list of resources provides further reading and in-depth understanding of PTSD.

- Organizations and Support Groups: Numerous organizations offer valuable support and services for individuals with PTSD.

Throughout this book, the focus has been on providing practical advice, tools, and resources to support individuals on their journey to recovery and fulfillment.

Reflecting on the Journey of Healing

The journey of healing from PTSD is unique to each individual. It involves navigating challenges, embracing resilience, and finding new paths to joy and fulfillment. Reflecting on this journey is an important part of the healing process.

Key Reflections:

1. Acknowledging the Struggles:
   - Facing Challenges: Healing from PTSD involves facing and overcoming numerous challenges. It is important to acknowledge the difficulties encountered along the way.
   - Recognizing Progress: Reflecting on the progress made, no matter how small, provides motivation and a sense of accomplishment.

2. Embracing Resilience:
   - Inner Strength: The journey of healing highlights the inner strength and resilience that individuals possess. Embracing this resilience is crucial for ongoing recovery.
   - Learning from Setbacks: Setbacks are a natural part of the healing process. Learning from these experiences strengthens resilience and fosters growth.

3. Finding Joy and Fulfillment:
   - Personal Growth: The journey of healing offers opportunities for personal growth and self-discovery. Embracing new interests and passions enhances joy and fulfillment.
   - Building Connections: Strong relationships and support networks provide essential emotional support and a sense of belonging.

4. Celebrating Milestones:

- Acknowledging Achievements: Celebrating milestones and achievements reinforces positive progress and encourages continued effort.

- Setting New Goals: Continuously setting and working towards new goals ensures ongoing growth and development.

5. Ongoing Journey:

- Continual Growth: Healing from PTSD is an ongoing journey. It involves continuous learning, adapting, and growing.

- Commitment to Well-Being: Prioritizing mental and physical well-being remains essential throughout the journey.

Reflecting on her journey of healing, Lisa realized how far she had come since her initial diagnosis. She acknowledged the challenges she faced and celebrated the progress she made in managing her symptoms. Lisa embraced her resilience and found joy in new hobbies and connections. Her journey was a testament to the power of reflection and the importance of celebrating milestones.

Reflecting on the journey of healing involves acknowledging struggles, embracing resilience, finding joy, celebrating milestones, and committing to ongoing growth. This reflection provides a sense of accomplishment and motivation for continued recovery.

Encouragement for Ongoing Resilience

Ongoing resilience is vital for managing PTSD and maintaining a fulfilling life. It involves developing and nurturing the ability to cope with challenges, adapt to changes, and continue moving forward.

Building Ongoing Resilience:

1. Developing Coping Strategies:

- Mindfulness Practices: Regular mindfulness practices, such as meditation and deep breathing, help manage stress and maintain emotional balance.

- Physical Activity: Engaging in regular physical activity improves overall well-being and reduces symptoms of anxiety and depression.

2. Seeking Continuous Support:
- Therapy and Counseling: Ongoing therapy provides continuous support and guidance for managing PTSD symptoms.
- Support Groups: Participating in support groups offers a sense of community and shared experiences, which can strengthen resilience.

3. Embracing Change:
- Adapting to New Normals: Being open to change and embracing new normals is crucial for ongoing resilience. This includes adjusting routines, coping strategies, and goals as needed.
- Exploring Opportunities: Seeking new opportunities for personal and professional growth fosters a positive outlook and a sense of purpose.

4. Maintaining a Positive Outlook:
- Gratitude Practices: Practicing gratitude by focusing on positive aspects of life and expressing appreciation enhances overall well-being.
- Reframing Challenges: Viewing challenges as opportunities for growth and learning encourages a positive mindset and proactive problem-solving.

5. Building Strong Relationships:
- Nurturing Connections: Maintaining strong relationships with family, friends, and community members provides essential emotional support.
- Engaging in Community: Participating in community activities and volunteering fosters a sense of belonging and purpose.

After years of managing PTSD, Daniel found that ongoing

resilience was key to maintaining his well-being. He continued to practice mindfulness and engage in physical activity, which helped him manage stress. Daniel also sought continuous support from his therapist and participated in a support group. Embracing change and exploring new opportunities, such as volunteering, provided Daniel with a sense of purpose. His positive outlook and strong relationships were vital in maintaining his resilience.

Ongoing resilience involves developing coping strategies, seeking continuous support, embracing change, maintaining a positive outlook, and building strong relationships. These practices support long-term recovery and fulfillment.

FINAL WORDS FROM THE AUTHOR

As we conclude this book, I want to extend my deepest gratitude to you for embarking on this journey with me. Writing "Winning Over Post Traumatic Stress" has been a profoundly rewarding experience, and I hope that the insights, tools, and stories shared within these pages have provided you with valuable guidance and support.

Reflections on Writing the Book:

1. Purpose and Vision:
   - Empowering Readers: My primary goal in writing this book was to empower individuals dealing with PTSD by providing practical advice, resources, and inspirational stories.
   - Fostering Hope: I aimed to foster hope and encourage resilience, showing that it is possible to turn adversity into opportunity and create a fulfilling life.

2. Sharing Knowledge:
   - Comprehensive Resources: This book includes a wealth of information on understanding PTSD, seeking diagnosis and treatment, and building a support network.
   - Personal Stories: The inclusion of personal stories highlights the strength and resilience of individuals who have successfully navigated their recovery journeys.

3. Encouraging Ongoing Growth:
   - Continual Learning: Recovery from PTSD is an ongoing journey that involves continuous learning, adapting, and

growing.

- Support and Connection: Building and maintaining strong support networks is essential for long-term resilience and well-being.

Final Words:

1. Believe in Your Strength:

- Resilience and Courage: Believe in your resilience and courage. You have the strength to overcome challenges and create a fulfilling life.

- Embrace Your Journey: Embrace your journey with compassion and patience. Each step forward is a testament to your determination and resilience.

2. Seek Support:

- Professional Help: Do not hesitate to seek professional help when needed. Therapists, counselors, and support groups can provide valuable guidance and support.

- Community and Relationships: Build strong relationships and engage with your community. Support from loved ones and peers is crucial for ongoing recovery.

3. Celebrate Progress:

- Acknowledge Achievements: Celebrate your milestones and achievements, no matter how small. Recognize the progress you have made and use it as motivation to continue moving forward.

- Set New Goals: Continuously set and work towards new goals that align with your values and aspirations. This keeps your journey dynamic and fulfilling.

4. Turn Adversity into Opportunity:

- Positive Mindset

: Maintain a positive mindset and view challenges as opportunities for growth and learning.

- Pursue Fulfillment: Seek activities and opportunities that bring joy and fulfillment. Discovering new passions can provide a sense of purpose and direction.

Thank you for allowing me to be a part of your journey. I hope that this book has provided you with the tools, resources, and inspiration needed to navigate your recovery and create a life of joy and fulfillment.

With gratitude and encouragement,

Dr Bhaskar Bora

INVITATION TO SHARE PERSONAL STORIES AND FEEDBACK

Your journey and experiences are invaluable. Sharing your story can inspire others, provide support, and contribute to the collective understanding of PTSD. I invite you to share your personal stories and feedback on this book.

Sharing Personal Stories:

1. Inspiration and Hope:
   - Your Journey: Your journey of resilience and recovery can provide inspiration and hope to others facing similar challenges.
   - Empowering Others: Sharing your experiences can empower others to seek help, embrace change, and pursue a fulfilling life.

2. Support and Community:
   - Building Connections: Sharing your story fosters connections within the community, creating a network of support and understanding.
   - Collective Wisdom: Your insights and experiences contribute to the collective wisdom and resources available to individuals with PTSD.

Providing Feedback:

1. Your Insights:
   - Reflections on the Book: Your feedback on this book is invaluable. I would love to hear your reflections on how the

content, resources, and stories have impacted you.

- Suggestions for Improvement: If there are areas where this book could be improved or additional topics that could be covered, please share your suggestions.

2. Ongoing Dialogue:

- Continuing the Conversation: Your feedback helps continue the conversation about PTSD, resilience, and recovery. It allows for the ongoing development of resources and support for the community.

- Engaging with Readers: Engaging with readers' feedback and stories fosters a collaborative and supportive environment for everyone involved.

How to Share:

1. Contact Information:

- Email: You can share your stories and feedback via email at bora.dr@gmail.com

- Online Community: Join our online community at www.thesecondchanceinlife.com
to connect with others, share your journey, and provide feedback.

2. Confidentiality:

- Privacy: Your privacy is important. You can choose to share your stories and feedback anonymously if you prefer.

- Respect: All shared stories and feedback will be treated with respect and confidentiality. Names will be changed to protect identity.

Your contribution is vital in supporting others and enhancing the resources available for individuals with PTSD. Together, we can create a community of resilience, understanding, and hope.

Final Invitation:

I invite you to share your personal stories and feedback. Your experiences and insights can inspire others, foster connections, and contribute to the ongoing dialogue about PTSD and recovery. Thank you for being a part of this journey.

ACKNOWLEDGEMENTS

Writing this book has been a journey filled with learning, growth, and deep reflection. I would like to extend my heartfelt gratitude to everyone who supported me throughout this process. First and foremost, I thank the countless individuals who shared their stories of resilience and recovery. Your courage and strength have been a profound inspiration. I am immensely grateful to my family and friends for their unwavering support and encouragement. Your patience and understanding have been invaluable. Special thanks to my colleagues and mentors in the field of mental health. Your expertise and guidance have enriched this book immeasurably. Finally, I dedicate this book to all those who are on their journey to healing from PTSD. May you find hope, strength, and the knowledge that you are not alone.

COPYRIGHT INFORMATION© 2024 DR. BHASKAR BORA.

LEGAL DISCLAIMER

The information provided in this book is for educational purposes only and is not intended as a substitute for professional advice, diagnosis, or treatment. The names of all people with personal stories have been changed to protect identities. Always seek the advice of your physician or other qualified health provider with any questions you may have regarding a medical condition. Never disregard professional medical advice or delay in seeking it because of something you have read in this book. The author and publisher make no representations or warranties with respect to the accuracy or completeness of the contents of this book and specifically disclaim all warranties, including without limitation warranties of fitness for a particular purpose. The advice and strategies contained herein may not be suitable for your situation. You should consult with a professional where appropriate. Neither the author nor the publisher shall be liable for any loss of profit or any other commercial damages, including but not limited to special, incidental, consequential, or other damages.